Clement of Rome
— & —
the Didache

A New Translation
and
Theological Commentary

KENNETH J. HOWELL

Early Christian Fathers Series: 2

CHResources

CHResources

PO Box 8290

Zanesville, OH 43702

740-450-1175

www.chnetwork.org

CHResources is a registered trademark of the
Coming Home Network International

Library of Congress Cataloging-in-Publication Data

Howell, Kenneth J. (Kenneth James)

Clement of Rome and the Didache : a new translation and theological
commentary / Kenneth J. Howell.

p. cm.

Includes bibliographical references(p.   ) and indexes.

ISBN 978-0-9830829-7-2 (alk. paper)

1. Clement I, Pope, d. ca. 99. 2. Clement I, Pope, d. ca. 99. Epistola ad
Corinthios. 3. Bible. N.T. Corinthians--Criticism, interpretation, etc-
-Early works to 1800. 4. Church history--Primitive and early church, ca.
30-600. 5. Didache. 6. Christian ethics--Early works to 1800. I. Clement I,
Pope. Epistola ad Corinthios. English. II. Didache. English. III. Title.

BR65.C56H69 2012

270.1--dc23

2012038689

Cover design and page layout by Jennifer Bitler www.doxologydesign.com

Ad redintegrationem unitatis
omnium Christianorum dedicatum

Table of Contents

Preface   i

A Note on Text, Translation, and Scholarship   v

Abbreviations   vii

INTRODUCTORY ESSAYS

Chapter 1: Clement of Rome and His *Letter to the Corinthians*   1

Chapter 2: Sedition and Schism in the Church of Corinth   13

Chapter 3: Structure and Authority in Clement's View
of the Church   23

Chapter 4: Clement's View of God and Christ   37

Chapter 5: Faith, Works, and Salvation in Clement of Rome   45

Chapter 6: The *Didache*: History and Literature   57

Chapter 7: The Theology of the *Didache*   67

TRANSLATIONS AND COMMENTARIES

Chapter 8: Clement of Rome's *Letter to the Corinthians*   79

Chapter 9: The Teaching of the Lord for the Nations through
the Twelve Apostles (The *Didache*)   137

Bibliography   153

Index of Principal Greek Terms   157

General Index   163

About the Author   187

Acknowledgements   189

On Reading Ancient Christian Writings

Clement of Rome's *Letter to the Corinthians* and the *Teaching of the Twelve Apostles* (the *Didache*) are unique among Christian writings. Of those that have survived antiquity, these are two of the most important writings for understanding Christianity in the second half of the first century. While no one can be absolutely certain of the dates of their composition, there is widespread agreement that they provide a unique window on the Christian church in the period soon after the New Testament. The only other documents that come close to their time are the seven letters of Ignatius of Antioch, which I made available in the first volume in this series. The purpose of these new translations and commentaries is to make direct contact with early Christian history possible for the educated non-specialist.

The letter of Clement to the Corinthians has been read, translated, and used by scholars for centuries, as has the *Didache* since its discovery in 1873, but the concerns of scholars are not always those of my intended readers. These two seminal documents are too important to be read only by scholars of ancient Christianity. They are presented here so that Christians of all stripes may reflect on their importance for the contemporary practice of the Christian faith at both a personal and an institutional level.

At the beginning of the third millennium of Christianity, there are compelling reasons to make available these early sources of the Christian faith, since there appears to be a renewed desire among Catholic, Orthodox, and Protestant believers to understand the history of their respective communions with regard to Christian antiquity. Many sense the relevance of that history for the articulation of the faith. All three traditions share common ground in the struggles, insights, and formulations of the first centuries of the church. The translations presented here seek to be fair to all Christians, and the interpretations, the introductory essays, and the commentaries are intended as an invitation for believers of all backgrounds to interact about the roots of their faith.

The desire for a greater unity among traditional Christians has always lodged in the hearts of the baptized, but the last thirty years have brought that desire into more visible form. Dialogue and understanding of different ecclesial communions has increased in ways that would have been unthinkable one hundred years ago. Yet, this laudatory development occurs at the same time that many communions are floating on a doctrinal sea without an anchor. Some in these communions are consciously attempting to redefine Christian belief and morals. Others, fixed in churches rooted in tradition, stand in disbelief as they view these developments. It raises the question of standards. How can we know what is within the proper boundaries of Christian faith? This volume, like the first in this series, is dedicated to the restoration of Christian unity (*ad redintegrationem unitatis omnium Christianorum*). But these translations are offered with the conviction that a greater unity, if it is to be truly Christian, must be rooted in the historic sources of the faith, both in Scripture and in the earliest Christian fathers.

However interpretations of these writings may differ, there can be no question as to their relevance and importance for our contemporary quest. I believe that every scholar has an obligation to divulge his leanings and inclinations. To do so, he must be hermeneutically self-conscious. I offer these translations, commentary, and interpretative essays with the awareness that my involvement in and commitment to the Catholic faith in union with the See of Peter has shaped my reading of Clement and the *Didache*. But what one brings to this reading does not have to prejudice the outcome. The text is there for all to investigate because ultimately meaning and interpretation are not arbitrary. They are discovered in the love and unity of the church, which reads earlier Christian history with a hope of passing on that faith to the next generation.

Kenneth J. Howell
23 November 2012
Memorial of St. Clement of Rome

A Note on Text, Translation, and Scholarship

I n a work directed to the educated non-specialist, it is neither possible nor desirable to treat all the questions one may ask. I have therefore assumed positions on certain questions that scholarly readers may doubt, but I do not think those assumptions injure the most important aspects of my interpretations. I have sought to assume only those points of debate that seem relatively settled among expert scholars.

Texts

For my translations, I have used standard modern editions of the Greek texts. While I do not assume that every textual variant chosen in modern critical editions is correct, I have largely taken the text used in Annie Jaubert's edition of *Clément de Rome*: Épitre *aux Corinthiens* in the Sources Chrétiennes series (no. 167) that was first published in 1971 and reprinted in 2000. From the same series, I have used Willy Rordorf's and André Tulier's *La Doctrine des Douze Apôtres* (no. 248bis) for the text of the *Didache*. These were put in digital form in the *Thesaurus Linguae Graecae* online.

Translation

I have sought to find middle ground in my translations between too literal and too free-flowing, though I probably lean more to the literal, with the belief that this allows the reader to decide on interpretative matters. The reader will note the use of brackets [...] means that the word(s) contained are not in the original Greek but are inserted because they are strongly implied or necessary for clarification. All Greek words are cited in their lexical form to facilitate readers who do not know Greek. Occasionally, I have cited words in their inflected forms if it is relevant to the point under discussion. The Greek index has the meanings of some of the more prominent terms. Like any translator, I have consulted with previous English versions, but I have also used the French translations of Annie Jaubert and Willy Rordorf and the Italian translation of Antonio Quacquarelli. My thanks to Colin Howell for his explanations of the Italian, and Marie Jutras for hers of the French.

Scholarship

I stand in a long line of scholars who have translated and interpreted these writings. The late nineteenth century witnessed a flourish of activity devoted to the apostolic fathers, from famous scholars like Adolf Harnack and Theodor Zahn. However, it is widely acknowledged that the master scholar of these earliest Christian writings was Joseph Barber Lightfoot, the Anglican bishop of Durham. Lightfoot left no stone unturned and wrote about every topic raised in these writings. All subsequent students of the apostolic fathers are indebted to him. In my commentary, I rarely mention Lightfoot, but my work, as with the work of others, would have been impossible without his. The names that appear prominently in my interpretative notes and essays are scholars from the 1960s and on, some of whom are Bart Ehrman, Robert Grant, Michael Holmes, Annie Jaubert, James Kleist, Aaron Milavec, Antonio Quacquarelli, and Willy Rordorf.

Abbreviations

References to biblical books will follow standard abbreviations in American English.

ABBREVIATIONS OF ANCIENT WRITINGS

ClCor   Clement's *Letter to the Corinthians*

Di   The *Didache*

PolyPhil   Polycarp's *Letter to the Philippians*

OTHER ABBREVIATIONS:

Ehrman   *The Apostolic Fathers*, ed. and trans. Bart Ehrman (Cambridge, MA: Harvard University Press, 2003)

Grant   Robert Grant, *The Apostolic Fathers: A New Translation and Commentary*, vol. 2, *First and Second Clement* (New York: Thomas Nelson & Sons, 1965)

Hemmer   Hippolyte Hemmer, *Clément de Rome: Épître aux Corinthiens et Homélie du IIe siècle* [Greek text, French translation, introduction, and index], Les Pères Apostoliques (Paris: Libraire Alphonse Picard et Fils, 1909)

Holmes   *The Apostolic Fathers: Greek Texts and English Translations*, ed. and trans. Michael W. Holmes, 3rd ed. (Grand Rapids: Baker Academic, 2007)

Jaubert   Annie Jaubert, *Épître aux Corinthiens* (Paris: Éditions du Cerf, 1971)

Kleist   James Kleist, *The Epistles of St. Clement of Rome and St. Ignatius of Antioch* (Mahwah: Paulist Press, 1946)

Lightfoot	J.B. Lightfoot, *The Apostolic Fathers: Clement, Ignatius, and Polycarp*, vols. 1 and 2 (Peabody: Hendrickson Publishers, 1989)
lit.	literal or literally
LXX	The Septuagint, the Greek translation of the Old Testament (ca. 250 B.C.)
MSS	manuscripts
MT	Massoretic Text (the standard Hebrew text of the Old Testament in use since about the ninth century)
NT	New Testament
OT	Old Testament
Quacquarelli	Antonio Quacquarelli, *I Padri Apostolici* (Rome: Citta Nuova Editrice, 1976)
Rordorf	Willy Rordorf and André Tulier, *La Doctrine des Douze Apôtres* (*Didache*), Sources Chrétiennes no. 248bis (Paris: Éditions du Cerf, 1998)

CHAPTER ONE

Clement of Rome and His *Letter to the Corinthians*

Readers of the New Testament have no trouble identifying Rome and Corinth as two of the most important cities in the times in which the apostles lived. Rome was the capital and center of a vast empire that had direct jurisdiction over and impact on the land of Jesus's birth and life. Paul, the apostle to the Gentiles, penned his letter to the Romans in anticipation of traveling to and through the great metropolis on his way to Spain "to preach the gospel where Christ had not been named" (Rom 15:20,24). The Acts of the Apostles, the earliest history of the church, relates how Paul ended up in Rome as a prisoner under house arrest awaiting his trial before Caesar (Acts 28:16-31). We know from Paul's Letter to the Romans that the church in Rome was already thriving in the fifties of the first century, but we know nothing of its origins or how the gospel came to the center of the empire. One thing is clear. Rome was unmistakably the most important city in the spread of the Christian faith to the Western world.

Corinth was a different city from Rome but equally important in the Greek-speaking East. From the pages of the New

Testament alone, we can learn much of the church in Corinth because of Paul's two lengthy letters. In First and Second Corinthians, we learn that living in Corinth was particularly difficult for the new Christian converts under Paul's ministry there. Corinth was a busy commercial center that served as a crossroads for many travelers. As the capital city of Achaia, Corinth was a place of significant influence, which was suffused with pagan religion and its accompanying immorality. All this was troubling for the fledgling church. Most of this can be inferred from the New Testament itself.

In addition to the New Testament, we have other sources from the early centuries of Christianity that tell us much about the churches in Rome and Corinth. As to Rome, these sources reveal that Clement, the third bishop of Rome after Peter, penned a very long letter to the Corinthian church, which was written sometime in the last decade of the first century (90-100 A.D.), about thirty years after the martyrdoms of Peter and Paul in Rome. As to Corinth, Clement's letter reveals a church facing problems not unlike those in Paul's day. There is much to learn about the existence of the church in a pagan society from both Paul and Clement. Understanding Clement's letter, however, requires an overview of its contents.

What Is the *Letter to the Corinthians* About?

The overriding concern in the *Letter to the Corinthians* has to do with schism and sedition. The church in Corinth seems to have been as troubled and divided in Clement's day as it was in Paul's. Approximately forty years separated their respective correspondence, but the old problems remained. Or maybe it is better to say that the old problems resurfaced. Division, schism, and sedition have plagued the church from its beginning to the present day. What then is the solution to these perennial problems, these devastating plagues? The answer lies in understanding the nature and structure of the church.[1]

---

1   The nature of the church as love is treated in more depth in chapter 2, and the

The church, according to Clement, is a community of love, peace, and hospitality. It welcomes all sinners and calls them to faith, repentance, and good works. The nature of the church is love, divine love manifested in Christ. The structure of the church is also divine. The origin of its structures is from the apostles, who received it from Christ himself.[2] The doctrine of apostolic succession, as outlined in chapters 42 to 44, constitutes the clearest statement of this teaching in the early church. Apostolic succession is the author's answer to the problems of schism and sedition. The order God placed in the church must be recognized and followed if there is to be no schism and rebellion in the body of Christ.[3]

However, to a modern reader, Clement is prolix and meandering in his statement of the problem and solution. Like many documents from antiquity, the *Letter to the Corinthians* seems to wander through topics that have little to do with the nature and structure of the church. But this is only true on a superficial reading. A profound underlying unity of the letter is there for those who wish to dig more deeply into it.

The letter begins by noting the problems of schism and sedition in chapter 1. Reports of schism and sedition stand in stark contrast to the glorious reputation of the Corinthian church. Although Clement praises the Corinthian Christians for rejecting schism and sedition in the past,[4] these twin evils have raised their ugly heads again, so much so that "the dishonorable rose up against the honorable, the inglorious against the glorious, the foolish against the wise, the young against the elders" (3:3). The author begins by citing examples of Old Testament figures who displayed jealousy and strife that ended in

---

structure of the church in chapter 3, of the introductory essays.

2   "The apostles received the gospel for us from our Lord Jesus Christ, and Jesus Christ was sent from God. So Christ was from God and the apostles from Christ. So both came by the will of God in good order" (*ClCor* 42:1).

3   The doctrine of apostolic succession is treated more fully in chapter 3 of the introductory essays.

4   "All disorder and schism were abominable to you" (2:6).

death (ch. 4). In chapter 5, the author shows that the martyr-doms of Peter and Paul displayed the same evils on the part of the Roman authorities. Those same tendencies to jealousy and strife, to schism and sedition, are present in the Corinthian church; none of this is the will of God (cf. 9:1).

As the author works his way through numerous examples from the Old Testament, he concludes with an exhortation, "So let us be humble, casting away all pride, blindness, foolish-ness, and wrath. Let us do what is written" (13:1). He reminds the Corinthians that "Christ is for those of a humble mind, not those who raise themselves over his flock" (16:1). Pointing to Christ as the meek servant of God who delivered himself up for our sins, the author proceeds to quote the entirety of Isaiah chapter 53 to demonstrate the servant-like attitude of Christ's true followers.[5]

In chapters 19 and 20, the author parades examples of God's orderly design of nature so as to say that God is always a God of order and never of disorder (cf. 1 Cor 14:33). From chapters 24 to 26, the author provides examples of God's ability to bring things back to life, taking examples from the natural cycles and even from Greek legend.[6] At times the author does offer stinging rebukes to his recipients,[7] but mostly he encourages his hearers to embrace the positive examples of God himself.[8] He exhorts the Corinthians to good works, while at the same time reminding them that they are saved, not by their works, but by the grace of God.[9]

---

5   We will examine Clement's theology of God and Christ more fully in the fourth chapter of the introductory essays.

6   See chapter 25, where Clement invokes the myth of the Phoenix to argue that the idea of a resurrection is not unknown, even among the pagans.

7   "Let us do everything consistent with holiness, fleeing evil speech, vile and unholy entanglements, drunkenness, along with youthful and disgusting passions. Let us flee foul adultery and abominable arrogance. For it says, 'God resists the proud but gives grace to the humble'" (30:1-2).

8   "Let us then approach him in holiness of soul, lifting up to him holy and spotless hands, loving our gentle and compassionate Father who has made us for himself as part of his election" (29:1).

9   See ch. 32 and 33.

Although every chapter in this letter is a treasure waiting to be explored, the most interesting section of the last part is in chapters 59 to 61, where the author seems to be quoting from a liturgy. Sections of these chapters have clear affinities with later liturgies and speak with language that has a definite liturgical flavor.

In all, the *Letter to the Corinthians* stands as a clear witness to the life of the early church within one generation of the apostles. It speaks in the vein of the New Testament of the evils of schism and rebellion against the legitimately ordained pastors of the church and calls all the faithful to obedience and holiness. Clement's view of the church rests on God's love and authority. The purpose of his letter is to restore unity, harmony, and order within the Corinthian church because these are the true features of the church in its nature and structure.

Clement of Rome's Letter in the History of the Early Church

Thus far I have spoken confidently of the *Letter to the Corinthians (First Clement)* as coming from the hand of Clement, the third bishop of Rome after Peter. Yet the fact remains that the letter does not mention Clement's name nor even that it is specifically from the bishop of Rome.[10] The Salutation simply says, "The church of God on its pilgrimage in Rome [writes] to the church of God on its pilgrimage in Corinth." How then did this letter come to be ascribed to Clement? The witnesses of history are abundant, and there is no detectable dissent from this view in any ancient Christian writings.

The most complete source of information about Clement's person and letter comes from Eusebius, the early-fourth-cen-

---

10 The intensive research conducted on the apostolic fathers in the second half of the nineteenth century generally led scholars to the conclusion that the homily known as Second Clement was not an authentic writing of Clement of Rome. Since that time, the document has been referred to either as "the so-called Second Letter of Clement" or simply as "A Homily from the Second Century." I concur with this scholarly consensus and will not treat that document in this volume.

tury bishop of Caesarea, who wrote one of the most important histories of the church up to his day. In his *Ecclesiastical History*, Eusebius draws on a now-lost history written in the second century by Hegesippus. Eusebius recounts that in the twelfth year of the emperor Domitian (A.D. 93), a man named Clement succeeded Anacletus as the bishop of Rome. He identifies this Clement with the man of the same name mentioned by Paul in Philippians 4:3, "With Clement and the rest of my coworkers whose names are in the book of life." Eusebius then speaks of the *Letter to the Corinthians*:

> There is one acknowledged letter from this man [Clement] that is great and amazing which he formulated as coming from the church of Rome to that of the Corinthians after sedition had taken place at that time among the Corinthians. We have learned that this letter was made public in many churches long ago and even now. And Hegesippus is a noteworthy witness that the Corinthians experienced this sedition.[11]

This brief mention shows that Clement's letter enjoyed wide and continuing circulation among the churches of various locales.

Later, Eusebius mentions the letter again in connection with *The Five Reminiscences* of Hegesippus, in which the latter recounts his travels to Rome:

> It is appropriate to listen to certain things said by him [Hegesippus] about the *Letter of Clement to the Corinthians*. He said these things, "And the church of the Corinthians remained in the orthodox doctrine [until the time of] Primus the bishop in Corinth. I mingled with the Corinthians on the way to Rome and spent some days among them during which time we were refreshed by orthodox doctrine."[12]

In the next chapter, Eusebius rehearses the ministry of Dionysius, the bishop of Corinth around 170. In one of Dionysius's letters addressed to Soter, the bishop of Rome at the same time, he mentions Clement's letter.

---

11   *Ecclesiastical History* bk. 3 ch. 15-16.

12   Ibid., bk. 4 ch. 22.

> In the same letter, he [Dionysius] recalls the Letter of Clement
> to the Corinthians, showing that it was a long-standing custom
> to read from this letter. He says in fact, "Today we spent the
> Lord's Day as a holy day in which we read your [Soter's] letter
> which we shall continue to read to be admonished as we do
> with the former one written to us by Clement."[13]

There are several important inferences we can draw from
Eusebius's account in his *Ecclesiastical History*. Although the
Letter to the Corinthians does not specifically say that it came
from Clement, Eusebius and the witnesses he cites testify that
it appears to have been universally, or at least widely, believed
to have come from him. As we shall see, Eusebius was not the
only church father who believed in Clement's authorship of
the letter. Was this widespread belief simply a tradition passed
down or was there a particular reason why this tradition was
handed on? If there was a reason, was it because of a desire to
ascribe the letter to some important figure of the past or because the author was the bishop of Rome? Secondly, although
Clement's *Letter to the Corinthians* was addressed to a specific
time and situation in Corinth in the last decade of the first century, later Christians took the letter as having a broader and
more enduring importance, much like the letters of Paul in
the New Testament. In Corinth itself, Dionysius's reading the
letter publicly some eighty years after it had been sent suggests
that the letter had an enduring significance. Was its perceived
significance because of the content of the letter; because the
problem of sedition, schism, and division was a perennial one;
because of the importance of the writer; or some combination
of these reasons?

Although Eusebius's *Ecclesiastical History* contains the
most complete information gathered in a single source from
the ancient church, Eusebius does not exhaust the evidence.
Another piece comes from Polycarp of Smyrna. That the *Letter to the Corinthians* was considered of wider importance
than simply a letter from one church to another surfaces in

---

13   Ibid., bk. 4 ch. 23.

the parallels scholars have discovered between Clement's letter and Polycarp's *Letter to the Philippians*, which some scholars have dated as early as 135.[14] Many scholars think that Polycarp possessed a copy of the *Letter to the Corinthians* because of the close parallels of phraseology. Anglican bishop J.B. Lightfoot was one of the first to detect striking similarities, a few of which are worth mention.[15]

1. APPEAL TO PAUL THE APOSTLE:
Polycarp: Neither I nor anyone like me is able to emulate the wisdom of the blessed and glorious Paul who, when he came among you in person, taught the message of truth accurately and firmly. When absent, he wrote you letters by which, if you studied closely, you can be built up further in the faith given you (*PolyPhil* 3:2).

Clement: Take up the epistle of the blessed Paul the apostle. What did he first write in the beginning of the gospel? In truth, he sent you a letter in the manner of the Spirit about himself, Cephas, and Apollos because at that time you created dissensions. But that dissension brought you a lesser sin, for you took the part of the attested apostles and of a man approved among them (*ClCor* 47:1-4).

2. EXHORTATION TO OBEDIENCE TO PRESBYTERS:
Polycarp: [I]t is necessary that those who are subject to the presbyters and deacons as to God and Christ abstain from all these things (*PolyPhil* 5:3).

Clement: [S]ubmit to the presbyters and allow yourselves to be instructed for repentance as you bow down the knees of your heart (*ClCor* 57:1).

---

14   A.D. 135 was the date assigned to Polycarp's *Letter to the Philippians* by Harrison, whose conclusions are favored by Jaubert. In any case, most scholars date Polycarp's martyrdom in Smyrna in the 150s. Given this, Harrison's supposition of 135 for the composition of the *Letter to the Philippians* is reasonable.

15   See Lightfoot, vol. 1, pp. 149-152. The parallels are more evident in the Greek texts of the respective letters.

3. MORAL EXHORTATIONS RELATING TO FAMILY RELATIONS:

Polycarp: Then also your wives [should remain] in the faith, love, and purity given to them by being affectionate toward their own husbands in all truth, and loving all equally with all self-control and to teach their children the instruction [coming from] reverence for God (*PolyPhil* 4:2).

Clement: The women you have commanded to conduct all their affairs in a blameless, devout, and pure conscience, each loving her own husband appropriately (*ClCor* 1:3). [L]et us instruct the young with training in the fear of God; let us help our wives to embrace the good (*ClCor* 21:6).

If, in fact, Polycarp's *Letter to the Philippians* was drawing on Clement's letter, it means that the latter was probably already in wide circulation in Asia Minor in the second quarter of the second century. Perhaps Polycarp's use of Clement's letter is an example of what Eusebius in the fourth century meant when he said, "We have learned that this letter was made public in many churches long ago."[16]

Another second-century witness is Clement of Alexandria, who quoted the *Letter to the Corinthians* extensively. The Alexandrian Clement quotes from the Roman Clement in his *Stromata*, book 4, chapter 17, when he is treating martyrdom. Four times the Alexandrian teacher specifically mentions Clement of Rome's name. Although we do not know the precise dates of the Alexandrian Clement's birth or death, we are certain that he worked in Alexandria in the last quarter of the second century and was therefore a contemporary of Irenaeus of Lyons.

It is in fact Irenaeus who gives us reason to believe that Clement's letter was held in such high esteem specifically because Clement was the bishop of Rome. Irenaeus's advocacy of Roman succession and primacy are well known to students of early Christianity. In *Against Heresies*, the bishop of Lyons re-

---

16   *Ecclesiastical History* bk. 3 ch. 15-16.

counts the primacy of the Roman church because of its being founded on the apostles Peter and Paul:

> For it is a matter of necessity, that every church [i.e., the faithful everywhere] should agree with this church [Rome] on account of its pre-eminent authority, inasmuch as the apostolic tradition has been preserved continuously by those [faithful men] who exist everywhere.[17]

As Irenaeus proceeds to list the succession of bishops in the Roman church down to his time, he specifically mentions both Clement and his *Letter to the Corinthians*:

> In the third place from the apostles Clement was allotted the episcopacy. This man, as he had seen the blessed apostles and had been conversant with them, might be said to have the preaching of the apostles still echoing [in his ears], and their traditions before his eyes. Nor was he alone [in this], for there were many still remaining who had received instructions from the apostles. In the time of this Clement, no small dissension having occurred among the brethren at Corinth, the church in Rome dispatched a most powerful *Letter to the Corinthians*, exhorting them to peace, renewing their faith, and declaring the tradition which it had lately received from the apostles, proclaiming the one God. ... From this document, whosoever chooses to do so, may learn that he, the Father of our Lord Jesus Christ, was preached by the churches, and may also understand the apostolic tradition of the church, since this Epistle is of older date than these men who are now propagating falsehood, and who conjure into existence another god beyond the Creator and the Maker of all existing things.[18]

What is striking about Irenaeus's account is that he was not writing a treatise about Clement or the Roman church per se, and yet he describes both the letter and Clement himself in words not applied to any of the other successors of the Roman See. Clearly for him, as for the other second-century witnesses, this letter was of abiding significance far beyond its time and its designated city of Corinth.

---

17   Irenaeus *Against Heresies* bk. 3 ch. 2.

18   Ibid., bk. 3 ch. 3.

The testimonies of Hegesippus, Dionysius of Corinth, Clement of Alexandria, and Irenaeus of Lyons leave us in little doubt that the *Letter to the Corinthians* was widely circulated and held as a great authority by the second half of the second century. Thus, within fifty to seventy-five years of its composition, the *Letter to the Corinthians* was held in high esteem in the ancient church from Alexandria and Asia Minor in the East to Lyons (ancient Gaul) in the West. Furthermore, this same letter was universally ascribed to Clement, the third bishop of Rome. Two possible reasons can be adduced for such widespread use; Irenaeus alluded to both these reasons indirectly. One is the belief that all the particular churches of the universal church must be united in doctrine and love. The witnesses cited earlier all sought a unity of doctrine in order to be both one and catholic (i.e., in union with the universal church). The second reason may be that a letter from the bishop of Rome had a special significance in the eyes of the other local churches because it was considered the mother church and the center of unity. This second reason, of course, has been heavily debated for centuries, because it lies at the core of present ecclesial differences among Protestant, Orthodox, and Catholic communions. Yet, all too often those differences are not stated with clarity. As we explore this letter, it is important to bear in mind that the *theological* content of Clement's *Letter to the Corinthians* may be interpreted and/or utilized in various ways today, but its *historical* reception in the ancient church leaves little room for doubt that the church fathers considered it a singular document with an importance far beyond its surface appearance.

CHAPTER TWO

Sedition and Schism in the Church of Corinth

O ne reason that Clement's *Letter to the Corinthians* was considered so important in the ancient church has to do with the nature of the problems it addressed. Clement's pastoral advice in the late first century did not occur in a vacuum, nor were the problems imaginations of the author. Like many of the letters in the New Testament, Clement's letter was occasioned by troubles and difficulties existing in the church at Corinth. As an occasional writing, however, Clement's letter can be situated in a historical context for which we have many more indicators than in other cases. Ignatius of Antioch, for example, penned seven authentic letters around A.D. 108, but we have no contemporary references to these letters, and all indications as to the historical problems must be inferred from the letters themselves. The same is true for the *Didache*. Only what is in the document itself will tell us of its origin, purpose, and character.

In the case of Clement, the situation is quite otherwise. Paul's two letters to the Corinthians and the Acts of the Apostles in the NT provide an abundance of historical information compared to that of Ignatius and the *Didache*. We will of course examine the internal clues within the letter itself, but these historical data from outside the letter set a context for understanding Clement's words.

The narrative of Paul's initial ministry in Corinth is recorded in Acts 18. Paul arrived in Corinth after his preaching of the gospel in Athens at the Areopagus. Luke, the writer of Acts, begins:

> After these things, Paul departed from Athens and came to Corinth. There he found a Jew by the name of Aquila, a native of Pontus, with his wife Priscilla. They had recently arrived from Italy because Claudius had ordered all the Jews to leave Rome. Paul came to them and because he was of the same trade as they, he stayed and worked with them. They were tentmakers. Every Sabbath, as he discussed things in the synagogue, he began persuading Jews and Greeks (Acts 18:1-5).

The chapter goes on to describe Paul's ministry in Corinth. Titius Justus, Crispus, and Sosthenes are mentioned among Paul's converts as he ministered there for a year and a half. The Jews attempted to have him arraigned before the Roman proconsul, Gallio, but the latter paid little attention to an issue that he perceived had to do with Jewish regulations more than with civil order. Paul's missionary activity in Corinth probably began soon after his arrival in Corinth during the late summer or early autumn of A.D. 50 since the emperor Claudius's decree expelling the Jews occurred no later than A.D. 49.[1] In any case, Paul's letters to Corinth reveal a church that was burdened by numerous problems.

Paul's Corinthian Correspondence

A few years later, in the 50s, Paul penned his First Letter to the Corinthians. From this letter, we can infer a multitude of problems that existed in the Corinthian church: schism and divided parties (1:10ff), open sexual immorality (5:1ff), attempts to settle disputes among Christians in the pagan courts (6:1ff), problems with marriage and consecrated virginity

---

1   See F.F. Bruce, *New Testament History* (New York: Doubleday, 1972), p. 298.

(7:1ff), liturgical abuses (ch. 11-14), doctrinal heresy (15:1ff), to name only some. In fact, in no other of Paul's letters does he touch on the same range of problems that is found in the Corinthian correspondence.

Particularly relevant to Clement's letter is the problem of schism that Paul addresses in chapter 1. Here Paul makes an explicit appeal to unity:

> I appeal to you, brethren, by the name of our Lord Jesus Christ that you say the same thing, and that there be no divisions [*schismata*] among you, that you be knit together in the same mind and in the same judgment. It was shown to me by Cloe's household that there are arguments among you. What I mean is that each of you says, "I am Paul's; I am Apollos's. I am Cephas's, I am Christ's." Has Christ been divided? Paul wasn't crucified for you, was he? Or you weren't baptized in Paul's name, were you? I am thankful that I baptized no one except Crispus and Gaius so that no one of you could say that you were baptized in my name (1 Cor 1:10-15).

Apparently, after Paul's initial missionary work in Corinth, Peter (Cephas) and Apollos of Alexandria had visited Corinth. After their ministries, members of the church began to form rival parties, each claiming the authority of their leader over the other ministers. This is also reflected in chapter 3:

> You are still of the flesh for where there is jealousy and strife, aren't you still of the flesh and live by human standards whenever someone says, "I belong to Paul"; another "I belong to Apollos?" Are you not mere men? What then is Apollos or what is Paul? They are servants through whom you believed. It is the Lord who gave each his own. I planted, Apollos watered, but God is the one who gave the increase. So, neither the one who plants nor the one who waters is anything, but God is the one who gives the increase. The one who plants and the one who waters are one. Each one will receive his own reward in accord with his labor. We are God's coworkers, you are God's field, his building (1 Cor 3:3-9).

It is significant that Paul mentions schism and division as the first of the many problems he addresses in Corinth. One might say that this problem is the root of all the others Paul later treats. For example, a careful reading of First Corinthians 10:14 through 14:40 suggests that there were severe divergences from the established liturgy that Paul had apparently left with them. In verse 10:14, Paul transitions from a discussion of participation in pagan worship to the eucharistic liturgy in the church. In 10:16-17, Paul asks two rhetorical questions to drive home the point of Christ's presence in the bread and cup used in the church's liturgy. Paul is reminding the Corinthians that their eucharistic liturgy is their new home of worship, not the pagan temples of Corinth.

When Paul returns to that same subject directly in 11:17ff, he now mentions divisions being manifested in the liturgy itself, "First of all, then, I hear that when you all gather as a church there are divisions [*schismata*] among you and I partly believe it." These divisions engendered disrespect for members of the church and debauchery (11:21). Paul's answer is to call the church back to its foundations in the liturgical tradition that he left them (11:23-26) and applies this tradition to instruct them in proper participation in the worship of the church. All this means that Paul's answer to schism and division is to call the church back to the apostolic foundation. We shall see something very similar in Clement's letter as well.

In chapter 12, Paul turns to abuses in connection with spiritual gifts. All too often Christians have read chapters 12 through 14 in isolation from chapters 10 and 11. However, Paul's discussion of spiritual gifts is tied to the abuses and correction of the liturgy by the call to unity. In chapter 12, Paul emphasizes that the diversity of gifts in the church is to be at the service of unity (12:4-11). I would like to point out two prominent themes that emerge in chapters 12 to 14. In both of these, Paul calls the church back to the moral foundation of love (ch. 13) and structural foundation of the offices that God has placed in the church (12:27-31) that insures orderly liturgy (14:26-38). Clement in fact follows Paul's example by emphasizing the same things.

Clement's *Letter to the Corinthians*

Clement possessed Paul's First Letter to the Corinthians and appealed to it as an authority. This indicates that Paul's letter(s) had circulated widely by the end of the first century and was considered, at least in Rome, as an authoritative part of the canon of the New Testament:

> Take up the epistle of the blessed Paul the apostle. What did he first write in the beginning of the gospel? In truth, he sent you a letter in the manner of the Spirit about himself, Cephas, and Apollos, because at that time you created dissensions (*ClCor* 47:1-3).

The problems within the Corinthian church that Clement wrote about in the 90s of the first century appear to be the same as those Paul addressed in the 50s. From the outset of his letter, Clement names sedition and rebellion as the cause. And with a vigor equal to Paul's, Clement condemns such divisive actions: "[W]e have more slowly turned our attention to those matters that are sources of strife among you, beloved, that is, of this unholy and profane rebellion [*stasis*][2] so foreign and alien to God's elect" (*ClCor* 1:1). Again in chapter 3, Clement enumerates the tragedy of schism and rebellion in contrast to the glorious foundation and growth of the church:

> All honor and expansion were given to you, but what was written has been fulfilled, "The beloved ate, drank, became fat, were fattened, and kicked back." From this come jealousy and envy, strife and sedition, persecution and instability, war and slavery. Thus, the dishonorable rose up against the honorable, the inglorious against the glorious, the foolish against the wise, the young against the elders. For this reason, justice and peace are absent (*ClCor* 3:1-3a).

The glorious beginning of the Corinthian church, founded as it was by the apostle Paul himself, gave way to indul-

---

2   I have sometimes translated the word *stasis* as "rebellion" and sometimes as "sedition." The word occurs nine times in Clement's letter, always with a negative connotation. The corresponding verb *stasiazo* ("to foment rebellion or sedition") occurs seven times.

gence ("The beloved ate, drank, became fat, were fattened, and kicked back"). The eight nouns Clement uses in 3:2 to describe what the church had become show a progressive descent into "slavery," which resulted from strife (*eris*) and sedition (*stasis*). Apparently, the Corinthian church had taken heed to Paul's admonitions because in 2:6 Clement said, "All disorder and schism were abominable to you," but this is quickly followed by the rebuke stated in chapter 3.

There does, however, seem to be a difference between Paul's and Clement's times. In Paul's letters, the problem was schism, divisions among the members of the church. In Clement's time, schism seems to have resulted from sedition, the overt rebellion of church members against established authority. *Schism* is the disintegration of fraternal bonds among the members of the church who form rival parties within it or new churches apart from the historic church. *Sedition* is open rebellion against the appointed leaders of the church in favor of some other leader or new doctrine. Schism and sedition are twin evils; they almost always go together. The gravity of sedition shows itself in chapter 14:

> It is just and holy, brothers, that we become obedient to God rather than to follow those leaders in the pride and instability arising from a foul jealousy. It is not an ordinary harm but a great danger to which we will be subject if we give ourselves over to the will of men who launch into strife and sedition to alienate us from the One who has our good in mind (*ClCor* 14:1-2).

Later, in chapter 46, Clement leaves us in no doubt about the results of these twin evils of sedition and schism: "Your schism has turned many away. It has thrown many into discouragement, many into disorder, and all of us into sorrow. Your rebellion [*stasis*] is persisting" (*ClCor* 46:9). That same chapter also offers the solution: it lies in the unity of God himself, "Why then are there strife, fights, divisions, schisms, and war among you?[3] Do we not have one God, one Christ, and one Spirit of grace poured out on us, and one calling in Christ?" (*ClCor* 46:5-6).

Images of the Church in Clement

The *Letter to the Corinthians* calls the church a pilgrim people in that each church is said to be "on its pilgrimage." In language reminiscent of Paul's first *Letter to the Corinthians* (see 1 Cor 1:2), Clement calls the Corinthians "those called, sanctified in the will of God" (Salutation). To be sanctified is to be set apart for the purpose of holiness, and so the metaphor of pilgrimage recalls that Christians are living in a country far from their true home.[4] As pilgrims in a foreign country, the members of the church form a place of harmony and peace.[5] The community that is formed in peace, harmony, and love is a place of hospitality like the examples of the same quality which Clement invokes.[6]

Clement's most gentle metaphor is that of the church as "the flock of Christ." He uses the phrase, or something similar, four times (16:1; 44:3; 54:2; 57:2), although he never speaks of Christ as shepherd (*poimen*). These four instances appear almost in passing as he is dealing with different subjects, but it is their apparent insignificance that reveals how Clement thinks of the church. In 16:1, he exhorts the Corinthians to humility by pointing to the humility of Christ himself:

> Christ is for those of a humble mind, not those who raise themselves over his flock. The scepter of God's majesty, the Lord Jesus Christ, did not come with vaunting ambition or ar-

---

3   See Jas 4:1.

4   Similar language is used in the NT by Peter, who speaks of Christians as "chosen sojourners of the diaspora" (1 Pet 1:1) and "pilgrims and sojourners."

5   Harmony (homonoia) occurs fifteen times, eight of which are used in a context of moral exhortation. Closely related is Clement's invocation of the harmony and peace of nature as an example for human harmony (see 20:10-11).

6   The word "hospitality" (*philoxenia*) occurs four times as a virtue connected with faith. See ClCor 1:2; 10:6 (Abraham); 11:1 (Lot); 12:1 (Rahab; cf. also 12:3).

> rogance, though he could have, but [he came] with humility, as
> the Holy Spirit spoke of him (61:1-2).

The remainder of chapter 16 consists of a quotation from Isaiah chapter 53 which, when applied to Christ, demonstrates not only his humble demeanor but also his humiliated life. Clement concludes the chapter with an exhortation of application, "See, O beloved, what model has been given to us! If the Lord humiliated himself in this way, what shall we do who have come through him under the yoke of his grace?" (16:17). Clement clearly teaches that being in "the flock of Christ" is a matter of taking on "the yoke of his grace." The yoke of Christ, of course, means following in the humble footsteps of Christ. So, for Clement, being a member of the flock means being yoked to Christ.

In chapter 54, Clement uses "the flock of Christ" in connection with the peace of the church. How can the peace of the church be restored and maintained? The key is to see it as God's flock ruled by properly appointed presbyters:

> Let him say, "if because of me there is dissension, strife, and schism, I will leave, I will go where you want, and I will do those things commanded by the congregation. Only let the flock of Christ live in peace with the appointed presbyters (54:2).

The one who is "noble, compassionate, and filled with love" (54:1) sees the harmony of the church as dependent on its having a proper structure and is willing even to absent himself if he becomes a source of dissension. So, in this context, "flock" connotes delicacy and vulnerability. Here the individual subordinates his own will and advancement to the peace of the church.

A similar context appears in chapter 57, where "the flock of Christ" surfaces once again. Here Clement contrasts self-seeking honor and recognition with smallness and insignificance "in the flock of Christ": "Learn to submit by casting off arrogance and the proud stubbornness of your tongue. It is better for you to be found small and accountable among the flock of Christ than to appear excellent and be cast away from his hope" (57:2). The member of the church who is willing to take his seemingly small place in the flock is in fact the one who should be honored. The flock is already viewed as insignificant in the eyes of the world. So being small and unnoticed in Christ's flock is a sign of true humility, the only real antidote to arrogance and self-will.

The last instance occurs in the context of Clement's chapter on apostolic succession (ch. 44). He speaks of those "who have ministered without blame to the flock of Christ with humility, quiet, and beyond-perfunctory service" (44:3). Humility, silence, and dedicated service are appropriate to the church because the flock is delicate and vulnerable. Serving the flock means having a disposition and demeanor corresponding to the place of the church in pagan society. These texts in Clement which contain references to "the flock of Christ" suggest that in Clement's mind two things are necessary for the church as the flock of Christ. One is respect for the proper structure of offices and authority; the other is to conduct oneself with humility and gentleness.

Clement's highest and most exalted answer to the problem of sedition and schism is love. Chapter 49 is his panegyric on love, modeled no doubt on Paul's famous love poem in First Corinthians chapter 13. Yet Clement's treatment of love differs from Paul's in that it follows more closely the rhetorical praise of his subject. Such a classical form typically began with rhetorical questions, reiterated at the close of the eulogy:

> Who can draw out the bond of the love of God? Who is sufficient to tell the greatness of his beauty? The height to which love leads is indescribable. … Beloved, see how great and wonderful love is; the perfection of love is beyond all telling (*ClCor* 49:2-3; 50:1).

Like Paul, Clement emphasizes that "love bears all things, endures all things," and that love is the opposite of arrogance (cf. 1 Cor 13:4-5). And as Paul stresses that love is what makes knowledge, prophecy, and sacrifice meaningful (e.g., 1 Cor 13:1-3), so Clement underscores that love excludes division and sedition, "Love does not contain division; love does not foment rebellion. Love does all things in harmony" (*ClCor* 49:5). But whereas Paul contends that love is the perfection of faith and hope (1 Cor 13:13), Clement points explicitly to Jesus Christ's sacrifice as the consummate expression of love (*ClCor* 49:6). In the end, both authors look to love as the answer to schism and the other problems facing the Corinthian church. Love is the animating force that enlivens the structure of authority within the church. Love does not replace structure or authority. Love expresses itself in obedience to the proper structures of authority. Yet neither authority nor structure is sufficient for church. Love must be their inner dynamic.

CHAPTER THREE

Structure and Authority in Clement's View of the Church

According to Clement's *Letter to the Corinthians*, the church is called to be a manifestation of the love of God in Christ. That love so permeates the body of Christ that the church becomes a place of harmony, peace, and hospitality. As the flock of Christ, the church lives under the guidance and care of the Good Shepherd (Jn 10:11). Schism and sedition have no place in the church; love always tends toward and demands unity.

The church, however, is more than a collection of believers or loosely organized congregations; it possesses a definite structure and order. Considerable evidence can be brought forth from the New Testament in support of this structure. But what is that structure? The question raises the matter of apostolic succession. Clement's *Letter to the Corinthians* is one of the earliest and most important witnesses we possess to the notion of apostolic succession and the primacy of the Roman church. Let us first examine apostolic succession.

Clement's fullest and clearest statement of apostolic succession occurs in chapter 44, but he adduces examples and illustrations of good order in earlier chapters to lend support to order in the church. This plan always consists of the elimination of jealousy and envy because the peace and harmony of the church are paramount.[1] But what order is necessary in order to keep unity and harmony in the church? To understand chapter 44, we must begin with chapter 42 of Clement's letter:

> The apostles received the Gospel for us from our Lord Jesus Christ, and Jesus Christ was sent from God. So Christ was from God, and the apostles from Christ. So both came by the will of God in good order. Once they received commands, once they were made confident through the resurrection of our Lord Jesus Christ, and once they were entrusted with God's word, they went out proclaiming with the confidence of the Holy Spirit that the kingdom of God would come. Preaching in lands and cities, by spiritual discernment, they began establishing their first fruits, who were bishops and deacons for future believers. And this was nothing new because for many ages it had been written about bishops and deacons, as Scripture says somewhere, "I will appoint bishops for them in justice and deacons in faith" (*ClCor* ch. 42).

According to Clement, the honor that the lay faithful owe to their pastors lies in the dignity of the offices that derive from Christ himself. In language reminiscent of Hebrews 2:3 ("salvation which at first was spoken by the Lord was confirmed to us by those who heard"), Clement ties together the preaching done by the apostles with the appointment of bishops (including presbyters) and deacons. He strengthens the connection between proclamation and church structure in chapter 44:

> Our apostles knew from our Lord Jesus Christ that there would be contention over the title of the bishop's office. For this reason, having received perfect foreknowledge, they appointed those mentioned before and afterwards gave the provision that, if they should fall asleep, other approved men would succeed their ministry. Now as for those appointed by them [the apostles], or by other men of high reputation with the approval

---

1   Clement regularly identifies the evils of jealousy (*zelos*) and envy (*phthonos*) as sources of the church's disharmony. See *ClCor* 3:2,4; 4:7-13; 5:2,4-5; 9:1; 14:1; 39:7; 43:2; 45:4; and 63:2.

of the whole church, that is, those who have ministered without blame to the flock of Christ with humility, quiet, and, beyond perfunctory service, those who are well attested by all for a long time, we do not consider it right to eject them from the ministry. It will be no small sin against us if we eject from the bishop's office those who have offered the gifts without blame and with holiness. Blessed are the presbyters who have gone before us who had a fruitful and perfect departure for they no longer run the risk of someone removing them from their established position. For we see that you have removed some who have ruled well from a ministry that is honored by their blameless lives (ch. 44).

Here Clement details the structure that gives stability to the church. It was the deliberate intention of the apostles to establish continuity in the church through a succession of offices. He links this foreknowledge to Christ by calling it "perfect." Apostolic succession consists of the endurance of an office and a procedure for filling that office. When he speaks of those "other approved men" who "would succeed their ministry," he is clearly stressing the continuity between the apostles themselves and their successors. The task of those who follow is clear; it is to continue and to advance the same ministry that they received. The procedure for filling the office consists of (1) a testing or probation of a man and (2) the approval of the whole church.

Clement does not cite any New Testament texts in support of his doctrine of apostolic succession. Why is this? Some would say that the New Testament contains no doctrine of apostolic succession, and therefore Clement had nothing he could cite. Others would say that apostolic succession was something passed on through oral tradition rather than written. Both views think the New Testament is silent about apostolic succession. The second view is more plausible given the evidence from ancient writers that Clement knew the apostles Peter and Paul.[2] I will argue below that neither of these is an

---

2   See the quotation from Irenaeus's *Against Heresies* bk. 3 ch. 3, quoted in chapter 1 above, on p. 10.

adequate theory because they both assume that the New Testament is silent about apostolic succession. As with so many other controversial subjects, how one interprets the New Testament evidence is crucial. Clement's lack of citing the New Testament in support of apostolic succession does not necessarily mean that the notion is absent from the New Testament.

If the New Testament does have indications of a doctrine of apostolic succession, why did Clement not cite that evidence in support? A reasonable hypothesis is that Clement did not need to cite it because the churches in Rome and Corinth already understood apostolic succession. The respective founders of each church — Paul in Corinth, Peter and Paul in Rome[3] — had already made that clear. If the churches had been taught verbally, then there would have been no need to cite textual support.

Are there any indications of apostolic succession in the New Testament?

One way to answer this is to read beneath the surface of the New Testament, so to speak, and discover if apostolic succession lies under its texts, that is, implied rather than expressed. One case is the election of Matthias in Acts 1:15-26. Here there is an awareness on the part of the nascent church of an apostolic vacancy that needed to be filled. Peter makes it clear in verses 16 to 19 that Judas had truly occupied an office in the apostolic band and that the Scriptures had predicted the need for "another to take his episcopacy" (v. 20b).[4] The prayer that accompanies their selection of Matthias (vv. 24-25) shows the church's awareness of divine guidance and choice.

Secondly, the remainder of the Acts of the Apostles confirms the idea of the appointment of ordained pastors for the

---

3   Of course, the church existed in Rome prior to Paul's and Peter's arrivals, as Paul's Letter to the Romans attests, but it was their apostolic presence which gave the church there its foundation. Their importance was no doubt the reason why the Roman church celebrates its founding on a feast day dedicated to Peter and Paul (June 29).

4   *episkope* has been translated "position of overseer" by the NRSV. I have translated the same word as "bishop's office" in *ClCor* 44:1.

expanding church. The appointment of presbyters was a part of establishing churches in the Gentile world (Acts 14:21-23). In Acts 20:17, Paul asks the presbyters of Ephesus to meet with him. Later, in his speech to them, Paul calls those who had been designated as presbyters, *episkopos* (overseers, bishops). From this text alone one might conclude that Paul did not distinguish between presbyters and bishops or that he was using the term *episkopos* to designate a function (overseeing) rather than an office. That may be, but it seems clear that the idea of passing on of an office with its functions was part of the early church's structure.

A third line of evidence comes from the Pastoral Epistles of Paul (1 and 2 Timothy, Titus). These letters, written toward the end of the New Testament era,[5] contain solid indications that succession of pastoral offices was a part of the original apostles's teaching. Paul explicitly left Titus on the island of Crete for the purpose of establishing an orderly structure for the church "by appointing presbyters in every city" (Tit 1:5). In 1:5, Paul calls these new pastors "presbyters," while in 1:7 he speaks of them as "bishops" (*episkopos*). Many read these references as Paul using the two terms interchangeably and therefore thinking that presbyters and bishops constitute one office. However, it is possible that Paul is thinking of two classes of pastoral leaders and simply specifying qualifications for both classes. Even then, these two offices do not have to be considered mutually exclusive since every bishop (*episkopos*) is also a presbyter, and every presbyter is potentially a bishop. If Paul is thinking of two offices instead of one, this would certainly mean that Ignatius of Antioch's clear distinction between the offices of bishop and presbyter was not a personal innovation but faithfulness to an earlier tradition. With either interpretation, however, the notion of a succession of offices seems clear.

---

5   I will not enter into the debate about whether the Pastoral Epistles were written by Paul. Nothing in my argument crucially depends on it. I will take as sufficient for my purposes the self-identification in the letters that specifies Paul (1 Tim 1:1; 2 Tim 1:2; Tit 1:1).

Paul ordained and authorized Titus, and he in turn would ordain and authorize others.

The word "bishop" is also used in 1 Tim 3:1-2, "If someone
longs [RSV has "aspires"] for the office of bishop [*episkope*],
he desires a good thing [RSV has "noble task"]. So a bishop
[*episkopos*] ought to be blameless … ". Paul then continues
to lay out qualifications for the office. The word "presbyter"
is used in that same letter in 5:17 and 19, where Paul is urg-
ing honor for the presbyters who rule well. The notion of a
body of presbyters surfaces in Paul's exhortation to Timothy:
"Don't neglect the gift [charism] which was given to you by
prophecy with the imposition of the hands of the presbytery"
(1 Tim 4:14). It is difficult with these occasional references to
know whether Paul is thinking of one office with two names
or two offices. But the pattern of passing on the faith and office
is clear. The conferral of a gift or charism comes through the
imposition of hands.

The passing on (*paradosis* or *traditio*) of an office and the
content of faith (*fides quae creditur*) does show up in other
contexts of the Pastorals. Paul invokes the notion of a deposit
of faith (*paratheke*) in 1 Tim 6:20, when he exhorts Timothy to
"guard the deposit" of faith. Again in 2 Tim 1:12-14:

> I know in whom I have put my trust and I am convinced that
> he [God] is able to guard my deposit until that day. Hold on to
> the pattern of sound words which you heard from me in the
> faith and love that are in Christ Jesus. Guard the good deposit
> through the Holy Spirit who dwells in us.

This deposit or "pattern of sound words" is spoken of in
other terms in 2 Tim 2:2 and 3:14.

With this practice of passing on an office as well as the
content of the gospel, Clement of Rome's belief in apostolic
succession seems more a matter of faithfulness to an earlier
tradition than a personal belief not shared by others. In the
sources cited in chapter 1 above, we saw how Hegesippus and
Irenaeus in the second century and Eusebius in the fourth believed in the notion of apostolic succession. Still, these were

later than Clement's time. Are there witnesses closer to his own time in the last decade of the first century? We can cite the letters of Ignatius of Antioch, who clearly understood the church to have a hierarchical structure. In his seven authentic letters, the bishop of Antioch — martyred most probably around A.D. 107 or 108, and so a contemporary of Clement of Rome — appeals to the divinely ordered structure of bishop, presbyter, and deacon:

> When you are submissive to the bishop as to Jesus Christ, you seem to me to be living not in accord with human custom but in accord with Jesus Christ who died for us. … [I]t is necessary to do nothing without [the approval] of the bishop, but to be submissive to the presbytery as to the apostles of Jesus Christ, our hope (*Letter to the Trallians* 2:1-2).

> All should revere the deacons as Jesus Christ in the same way that the bishop is the exemplar of the Father, and the presbyters are like the council of God and like the bond of the apostles. Apart from these a church cannot be called a church (*Letter to the Trallians* 3:1).

> Guard against such people. This will be [true] for you when you are not puffed up and are inseparable from God, i.e., Jesus Christ, the bishop, and the orders of the apostles (*Letter to the Trallians* 7:1).

> You all should follow the bishop as Jesus Christ does the Father. Follow too the presbytery as the apostles, and honor the deacons as the command of God. Let no one do anything that is proper for the church without the bishop. Let that Eucharist be considered valid [confirmed] that is under the bishop or performed by one to whom he entrusts it. Wherever the bishop appears, let there be the fullness [of the church] as wherever Christ Jesus appears, there is the catholic church. It is not lawful to baptize or to hold an agape feast without the bishop (*Letter to the Smyrneans* 8:1-2).

These quotations from Ignatius indicate his conviction that the governmental structure of the church (bishops, presbyters, deacons) is of divine origin and authority. There are no documents contemporaneous with Ignatius to countermand his hierarchical structure. As he addressed his letter to various churches of Asia Minor (Ephesus, Philadelphia, Smyrna, etc.), he always refers to their leader as bishop. While Ignatius does not specifically say that he believes in apostolic succession, his view of the hierarchical structure of the church is certainly consistent with Clement's teaching.

When considering the second question of Roman primacy and authority, scholars tend to divide into two camps. A minority of present-day scholars sees Clement's letter and other attesting sources (e.g., Irenaeus) as representing the mainstream view of ancient Christians that the Roman church was understood as the primary and leading church of the empire. Within this group, some think it was a primacy of honor and jurisdiction, while others see only a primacy of honor. These scholars tend to see confirmation of their view in Clement. However, the majority of present-day scholars in the West tend toward the view that belief in the primacy of the Roman church was simply one among many views present in the ancient church. This perspective tends to view ancient Christianity in general as having diverse creeds, forms of worship (liturgy), practices of piety, and even moral guidelines.

One of the more extreme representatives of this view is Bart Ehrman, who tends to see multiple Christianities in the ancient world, many of which have been lost.[6] For Ehrman, early Christianity was characterized by a great diversity of beliefs, practices, and pieties. When treating Clement and his letter, Ehrman expresses grave doubts about this letter coming from Clement or even from a chief bishop of the church of Rome:

> The letter of 1 Clement is the first surviving instance in which this church [Rome] attempts to extend its influence over another Christian community. To be sure, there is no indication of the hierarchical structure and efficient organization that would become characteristic of the church in Rome: no single bishop, let alone a pope, for example, at the top of a rigid eccle-

6   Bart D. Ehrman, *Lost Christianities* (Oxford: Oxford University Press, 2003).

siastical structure. Nor does the author or the church he represents stake any theological claim to personal authority. Instead the letter uses rhetorical techniques, scriptural precedents, and reasoned arguments to establish its position.[7]

While Ehrman acknowledges that this letter attempts to extend the influence of one church to or over another,[8] his choice of words ascribes to the later Roman church attributes which it has rarely or never claimed. When he cites the lack of any rationale based on "personal authority" — as if appeals to personal authority would characterize the later Roman church — he fails to comprehend that the bishop of Rome has never understood his authority to rest in the receptacle of his person. Documents issued by the bishop of Rome, from ancient to modern times, have always appealed to the office as the successor of Peter, not to the person of the officeholder.

The question of the authority of the Roman bishop, and therefore of the Roman church, remains. What authority, if any, did ancient Christians believe the Roman church had? And if the Roman bishop understood his church to have primacy over other churches, why does Clement not appeal to that authority? Or does he in implicit ways? Does the authority of the Roman church have anything to do with apostolic succession, which is clearly taught in chapter 44? The ecumenical implications of these questions are evident.

Perhaps the best place to begin is not with modern reconstructions of ancient Christianity but with the testimony of the ancients themselves. How did they understand the church and its structure? Earlier I cited letters of Ignatius of Antioch as evidence that apostolic succession may have been more widespread than in Clement's letter. But the one church Ignatius addresses that is not in Asia Minor, the church of Rome, has a slightly different tone from that in the other six letters:

---

7   Bart Ehrman, "Introduction to 1 Clement," in the *Apostolic Fathers*, Loeb Classical Library (Cambridge: Harvard University Press, 2003), p. 27.

8   Ibid.

> This church [Rome] has been loved and enlightened in the will of him who willed all things that exist in accord with the faith and love of Jesus Christ, our God. Your church presides in the region of the Romans; it is worthy of God, worthy of propriety, worthy of blessing, worthy of praise, worthy of success, worthy of purity and presiding in love, named by Christ, named by the Father (*Letter to the Romans*, Salutation).

Here Ignatius lists a number of praiseworthy attributes that he does not apply to the other churches. Most interesting is his statement, "your church presides in the region of the Romans" and his further phrase "presiding in love."[9] Since these are only passing references, it is not possible to insist on one understanding of Ignatius on this matter, but his phraseology is certainly consistent with the notion of the primacy of the Roman church. Thus, while Ignatius cannot be said to *teach* Roman primacy, his language *is consistent* with it.

The testimony of the ancients with regard to Roman primacy extends beyond Ignatius. The church in Corinth seemed to recognize the authority of Clement and the Roman church. If so, then Clement would not have needed to appeal to his or the church's authority. Such an appeal would have been superfluous. Is there any evidence to support this? Perhaps the answer lies in the same direction that we discussed in chapter 1 above of the introductory essays, when discussing authorship. There I noted that the *Letter to the Corinthians* was certainly taken to be Clement's by other bishops, including the later bishops of Corinth (Primus and Dionysius) in the second century. So, even though the text of the letter itself does not specify that it came from Clement's pen, other writers attest to it. But do we have similar evidence with regard to Roman primacy?

---

9   Elsewhere, I have discussed various interpretations of this phrase. See my *Ignatius of Antioch and Polycarp of Smyrna: A New Translation and Theological Commentary* (Zanesville, OH: CHResources, 2009), pp. 43-46.

At least two pieces of evidence are available, one direct, the other suggestive. Writing around A.D. 180, Irenaeus of Lyons testifies to a wider belief in Roman primacy:

> Since, however, it would be very tedious to reckon up the successions of all the churches, we do put to confusion all those who assemble in unauthorized meetings. We indicate that tradition derived from the apostles, of the very great, the very ancient, and universally known church founded and organized at Rome by the two most glorious apostles, Peter and Paul, as also [by pointing out] the faith preached to men which comes down to our time by means of the successions of the bishops. For it is a matter of necessity that every church should agree with this church, on account of its pre-eminent authority, that is, the faithful everywhere should do so inasmuch as the apostolic tradition has been preserved continuously by those [faithful men] who exist everywhere.[10]

Here is a bishop in Gaul (France) who had been raised in the East (Smyrna) and, when a boy, had heard Polycarp preaching. In other words, he has been exposed to the width and breadth of the church across the empire. In a manner that does not seem contrived or innovative, Irenaeus testifies to the "pre-eminent authority" of the Roman church on the grounds that it had been founded by Peter and Paul as well as because that church had preserved apostolic tradition. These grounds imply, as Irenaeus clearly says, that "it is a matter of necessity that every church should agree with this church [Rome]."

As we noted in chapter 1, Irenaeus listed the bishops of Rome from Peter down to his own time — when Eleutherius held the apostolic chair — with special emphasis on Clement. In the long passage from *Against Heresies* (bk. 3 ch. 3) cited above in chapter 1,[11] Irenaeus understands Clement's letter as an exercise of authority that the Roman church rightfully had. "This document," Irenaeus argues, presents the apostolic tradition that was by his time old. So, a non-Roman bishop in the

---

10   Irenaeus *Against Heresies* bk. 3 ch. 3 sec. 2.

11   See p. 10 above.

West, Gaul, who hails from the East, Smyrna, and therefore must have spoken both Latin and Greek, was in a position to know the faith of the church in the last quarter of the second century. We may read Irenaeus as expressing his own individual beliefs, or as he seems to have wanted to be understood, as representing the faith of the whole church.

There is other corroborating evidence as well. The material from Irenaeus that I have just given was thought to be important in the early fourth century, when Eusebius of Caesarea wrote his *Ecclesiastical History*. In book 5, Eusebius recounts the story of how Irenaeus became bishop of Lyons in 177 after the martyrdom of Pothinus his predecessor, and quotes from *Against Heresies* with the list given by Irenaeus.[12] This suggests that Eusebius agreed with and was following Irenaeus still in the fourth century. Further, in book 4, Eusebius relates the ministry of Dionysius of Corinth and the many writings he produced to help other churches.[13] Like later bishops who would write festal letters at Easter or communicate with dioceses other than their own, Dionysius did much to foster peace and unity in the church beyond Corinth. If this was already a common practice in the time of Dionysius — the second century — the practice could certainly have reached back to the time of Clement. If so, the bishop of Corinth in Clement's day, whoever he was, would not have found Clement's intervention objectionable. In fact, Eusebius quotes from Dionysius's letter to Soter, then bishop of Rome, that "the custom of the Romans is guarded even down to our day." What was that custom? "To benefit all brothers [i.e., Christians] in many churches" in both material and spiritual ways. And Dionysius tells Soter that they read his letter to the Corinthian church as well as "the one formerly written by Clement."[14] So, Clement's interven-

---

12 *Ecclesiastical History* bk. 5 ch. 6.

13 Unfortunately none of Dionysius's writings have survived.

14 The quotations in the last few sentences all come from Dionysius *Letter to Soter* bk. 4 ch. 23.

tion into the affairs of the Corinthian church does not seem unwelcome or unusual in the light of these ancient practices.

Finally, Eusebius indicates the enduring significance of Clement's letter in book 3:

> [T]here is one acknowledged letter of Clement that is great and amazing which he formulated to the Corinthians as if coming from the Roman church, at the time when there was dissension among the Corinthians. We know this letter has been publicly read in many churches both long ago and even now in our time. And Hegesippus clearly shows that there was dissension among the Corinthians.[15]

This demonstrates that, as late as the early fourth century, Clement's letter was still important. It could certainly have been because, as Eusebius explicitly says, it was a "great and amazing" letter. But for Dionysius — and perhaps for Eusebius — it was a means of preserving "the custom of the Romans."

Several firm conclusions arise from viewing Clement in the wider landscape of early Christian documents. In Clement, there is no inherent tension between the church as organism and the church as organization. The church has at once structure and vitality. Its life flows from the love of God made known in Christ but its structure guides the proper expression of that love. Both love and structure are gifts of Jesus Christ, and they are preserved by the passing on of the structure of apostolic succession. Love as the inner dynamic of the church, its soul as it were, tends toward harmony and unity. A church not in union with itself or with other churches is not a church governed by love. Love always tends toward unity. But in the material world where the historical church lives, there must also be a center of unity so that love can move toward its perfection. Perhaps that reality explains why Clement wrote to the church of Corinth.

---

15   *Ecclesiastical History* bk. 3 ch. 16. Translation mine.

CHAPTER FOUR

Clement's View of God and Christ

T he reason the church must be a communion of love is because God is love (cf. 1 Jn 4:8). The reason that the church must have a structure is because God is a God of order (cf. 1 Cor 14:33). The church's nature and being are ultimately grounded in God. Clement of Rome views God as Creator, Master, and all-Powerful Sustainer, but he also sees him as a compassionate Father who loves his creation and provides his church with the grace necessary for salvation. In this chapter, we explore more fully Clement's view of God and Christ.

God the Almighty Father

Drawing extensively on the Greek version of the Old Testament, Clement seeks to reinforce a continuity between Israel of the old covenant and the church of the new covenant. In Clement's *Letter to the Corinthians*, the appellation of "God" (*theos*) is always applied to the Father and never to Jesus.[1] The most common title applied to God is that of "Master" (*despotes*). Among the twenty-four occurrences of the word, the

---

1   But in keeping with the NT usage, Jesus is often called *kurios* ("Lord") in Clement.

most illuminating have to do with God's creative power. In chapter 20, the title is conjoined with Creator (*demiourgos*):

> The ocean that is boundless for men and the worlds beyond it are set right by the same orders of the Master … It is all these things that the great Creator and Master has fixed to exist in peace and harmony, showing kindness in them abundantly for us who have taken refuge in his mercies through our Lord Jesus Christ. To him be glory and majesty forever and ever. Amen (20:8,11-12).

Both titles of Creator and Master tell of the majesty and transcendence of God, who reigns as sovereign above his creation. Both indicate how the providence of the Almighty guides the course of nature and history, a truth made even clearer in chapter 24:

> The sower went out and cast each of the seeds into the ground. These seeds, falling into the dry and barren ground, are dissolved. Then, from this dissolution, the majesty of the Master's providence makes them arise and from one seed more grow and bear fruit (24:5).

The same two titles then naturally reflect the Genesis account of God's joy over all his works: "The Creator and Master of all rejoices over all his works" (33:2).[2]

Clement's letter also points to the transcendence of God, especially as it is found in the liturgical portion, chapters 59 through 61:

> You who alone are the Most Exalted in the heights, …
> [H]oly among the "holy ones" …
> Observer of human works …
> The Creator and Overseer of every spirit (59:3).

> For you have made clear the everlasting structure of the
>   cosmos through the things made.
> You, O Lord, created the inhabited world …
> wise in creation and sagacious,
> establishing what has come to be (60:1).

---

2   See Gen 1:4,10,12,18,21,25,31.

This sampling from Clement's prayer shows how he thinks of God as transcendent, but perhaps the most forceful statement of the sovereign, all-powerful, and all-mighty God comes in chapter 52, when he says, "the Master of all lives without need of anything. He needs nothing from anyone except that they would confess him" (52:1). The true God is so utterly other that every human thought of him fails to capture his essence. Clement's God is the same as the Holy One of the Old Testament: the all-Sufficient Master, Creator, and Providential Ruler. The God whom he proclaims and worships is transcendent and sovereign but not distant and uninvolved.

When Clement speaks of God as Father, he shows the loving nature of God. To be sure, God is "the Creator and Father of the ages, the all-holy One," but he shows his love through condescension. The word "condescension" has evolved in twentieth-century English into an almost entirely negative meaning, but its root meaning carries positive connotations as well. Coming from the Latin, "condescension" consists of the root *descendere* "coming down" and a preposition *con* "with", together meaning "coming down to be with." The Latin word translates *sugkatabasis*, a word loved by Christian authors writing in Greek to press home the same truth that the God of Christians is not a distant Deity who cares little for his human creatures. In Clement's letter, God condescends to our lowliness to be our Helper and Protector (59:4) who has "taught, sanctified, and honored" us (59:3). God is the protector of the lowly, the sick, the hungry, and the One who grants forgiveness (60:1-2).

All this becomes clear through his use of the term Father.[3] In chapter 23, Clement speaks of God's love as gentle and mild:

> The all-merciful and kind Father has compassion on those who fear him, distributing his graces gently and mildly to those who come to him with a simple mind. So, let us not be

---

3   The word "father" is used fourteen times by Clement; some instances refer to human fathers or progenitors (e.g., Adam, Abraham) while seven instances refer to God as Father.

> double-minded, nor let our soul dream up fantasies about his
> superabundant and glorious gifts (23:1-2).

The only appropriate response to such a kind and merciful Father is to love him with the whole of one's being, an exhortation that Clement arrives at in 29:1: "Let us then approach him in holiness of soul, lifting up to him holy and spotless hands, loving our gentle and compassionate Father who has made us for himself as part of his election."

So, in Clement's theology, he teaches God's power, sovereignty, and lordship in order to stress divine transcendence, but he stresses divine condescension in order to teach God's loving involvement with humanity. And in Clement's way of thinking, the mighty and all-powerful God expresses his condescending love most perfectly in Jesus Christ.

Jesus Christ, the Manifestation of Divine Love

Jesus Christ is the perfect expression of God's love. Christ is the Lord and Savior of the church. As we saw above in chapter 2, the church is a community of love because Christ dwells in the church. Among many means of speaking of Christ, Clement draws our attention to Jesus as the high priest of the new covenant people of God.[4] Drawing this title from the Letter to the Hebrews, Clement surrounds the term "high priest" with other titles that aid our understanding further: "This is the way, beloved, in which we found our salvation, Jesus Christ, the high priest of our offerings, the protector and helper of our weakness" (36:1). Here is a clear allusion to Hebrews 2:17, "that he [Jesus] may be a merciful and faithful high priest in what pertains to God so that he make atonement for the sins of the people," and also to Hebrews 4:15, "We do not have a high priest without the ability to sympathize with our weaknesses." However, Clement first calls Jesus Christ simply "our

---

4   "high priest" (*archiereus*) occurs five times in the letter. Two instances (40:5; 41:2) refer to the high priest of the OT. The other three refer to Jesus Christ as high priest.

salvation," then the "protector and helper of our weakness." Like the author of Hebrews, Clement sees the essence of our salvation as the help that Jesus gives to the church, a help made possible by the intercession that the high priest performs. By using the phrase "high priest of our offerings," Clement places Christ's priesthood in a context of the church's worship:

> Through him we fix our gaze on the heights of heaven.
> Through him we contemplate as in a mirror his unblemished and incomparable countenance.
> Through him the eyes of our heart have been opened.
> Through him our unenlightened and darkened understanding shoots up toward the light.
> Through him the Master willed for us to taste of immortal knowledge.
>
> He is the outshining of the Father's majesty and, inasmuch as he is greater than the angels, he has inherited a much better title[5] (36:2).

Since the language of worship is much like poetry, 36:2 suggests a liturgical context by the repetition of the phrase "through him" (i.e., Jesus Christ). Clement, then, thinks of Jesus Christ as opening up "the heights of heaven" and even allowing the church to gaze into the face of God. Such illumination is possible *because* Jesus is the true high priest of the church. Clement sees the church as the continuation and extension of Israel, the ancient people of God, the reason why he so clearly uses the levitical order in the Old Testament to justify the ministry of presbyters in the church. For him, the presbyters are the extension of the Old Testament priesthood, with Jesus Christ being the high priest of the new covenant.

The two other references to Jesus Christ as high priest appear to be titles that may have been standard in the Roman liturgy, "the high priest and protector [of our souls], Jesus Christ" (61:3; 64:1). The combination of "high priest" and "protector" points to the cure of souls which Christ gives the church:

---

5   This last sentence is taken from Heb 1:3-4. See my commentary.

> [M]ay the all-seeing God and Master of spirits and Lord of all
> flesh, who chose the Lord Jesus Christ and us through him to
> be a special people, may he give to every soul that is called by
> his majestic and holy name faith, reverence, peace, endurance
> and longsuffering, self-control, purity, and discretion so as to
> please his name through our high priest and protector, Jesus
> Christ. Through Christ is glory and majesty, power and honor
> to him [Father] now and forever and ever (64:1).

Christ's priesthood is ultimately the means by which the
church receives all the virtues listed in chapter 64. Christ's
priestly protection of souls opens heaven for the church and
guards it against defection.

Jesus Christ, being the high priest of the new covenant, has
to have blood to offer. And like the author of Hebrews, Clement associates the "blood of Christ" with his priesthood. For the
biblical author, the blood of the cross "cleanses the conscience
from dead works" (Heb 9:14) and gives "confidence for entry
into the holy place" (Heb 10:19); that same blood of Christ is
called "the blood of the covenant" (Heb 10:29) and "the blood
of the eternal covenant" (Heb 13:20). And that blood of Christ
is what "sanctifies the people" (Heb 13:12).[6] For Clement, the
blood of Christ is what redeems believers and gives them hope
in God (12:7; 49:6). The shedding of blood was foreseen in
the Old Testament in an unexpected way, that is, in the scarlet
cord hanging from Rahab's window (12:7). In citing the story
of Rahab told in Joshua chapter 2, Clement is showing the importance he attaches to Christ's blood. Here is the first known
instance in the history of Christian interpretation of the Old
Testament that sees the color of Rahab's rope as a harbinger of
Christ's redemption.[7]

Two particular occurrences of blood are striking. In chapter 49, Clement stresses the motivation for Christ shedding
his blood for the church. That motivation is love: "It is in love

---

6   In addition to Hebrews, the expression "the blood of Christ" or similar locutions
    occurs in the NT in 1 Cor 10:16; 11:27; 1 Pet 1:2; 1:19; and 1 Jn 1:7, among other
    places.

7   See also the commentary at 12:7.

that the Master has taken us to himself. It was because of the love that he had for us that Jesus Christ, our Lord in the will of God, gave his blood in our behalf. He also gave his flesh for our flesh, and his soul for our souls" (49:6). This statement occurs at the end of Clement's praise (panegyric) of love. His explanation of Christ's death as "his flesh for our flesh, and his soul for our souls" may be more than rhetorical flourish. It suggests that for Clement, Christ's death is a total gift of self. Our bodies and souls needed to be redeemed, and therefore, in God's economy of salvation, Christ gave both his body and soul for our redemption. This is all summarized under the phrase "gave his blood in our behalf." Pouring out his blood on the cross is Christ's way of giving his total self.

The last reference to blood in Clement's letter introduces connections not made in the New Testament. In exhorting the Corinthians, the author speaks of gazing upon the blood of Christ: "Let us fix our sights on the blood of Christ and know how precious it is to his Father. Because having shed it for our salvation, he brought the grace of repentance for the whole world" (7:4). The verb used is *atenizo*, which means "to stare, to gaze, to fix one's eyes." What could this possibly mean? How does one gaze upon Christ's blood which was shed far away from the Corinthians and Romans long ago? There may be here an allusion to the liturgy of the Eucharist celebrated in both churches. This visual allusion would make sense if the people of the church viewed the chalice (cup) of Christ's blood every Sunday at the elevation. We noted above how 36:1 suggests that Christ is the principal celebrant of the church's liturgy when it speaks of Jesus as "the high priest of our offerings." Since Christ is both priest and victim, the mention of gazing (*atenizo*) on the cup would mean that Christ's blood is the power for moral living. The verse quoted suggests why Clement would appeal to such an experience. Gazing on the blood of Christ in the liturgy reminds the laity of the relationship between the Father and the Son. The Father accepts the Son's sacrifice since "it is precious to his Father." And the realization that the church is accepted in the Son's sacrifice stirs the people of God to repentance. That repentance was won in Christ's bloody sacrifice; now the church can find repentance through gazing on the unbloody sacrifice of the Eucharist.

CHAPTER FIVE

Faith, Works, and Salvation in Clement of Rome

hroughout the *Letter to the Corinthians*, Clement of Rome speaks of faith, works, and salvation. While such language is not surprising for a Christian bishop, Clement's teachings have been variously interpreted by scholars. Some find a different and contradictory conception of salvation from Paul's, while others see an underlying harmony with the New Testament as a whole. No one doubts that Clement's language can at times appear to be at odds with that of Paul, but that same problem appears in reconciling James and Paul on justification within the pages of the New Testament itself. Clement, unlike Paul and James, never addresses the subject of justification directly, but his discussion of other subjects clearly presupposes some definition of faith and personal salvation that we must uncover.[1]

---

1   The German scholar R. Knopf, in his 1920 commentary on Clement, contrasted Paul's *sola fide* (by faith alone) to Clement's synergistic view of salvation. See Kleist's note (p. 110, n. 95) where he disagrees with Knopf's interpretation. Jaubert does not see Clement as contradicting Paul but also views him more in the Jewish wisdom tradition that understands all of creation and salvation as a gift. For her, Clement is closer to the teachings on faith implied in Heb 11.

Clement's concept of faith is expressed in language distinct from Paul and James. The noun "faith" (*pistis*) occurs nineteen times[2] in Clement's letter, while the verb "believe" (*pisteuo*) occurs only five times,[3] only three or four of which clearly refer to faith in the subjective personal sense. But this lack of emphasis on faith is only apparent, for Clement uses a wide range of other vocabulary to express the essence of faith. If we read Clement's letter with a wider lens, we see that faith means accepting God's will, that is, the order of salvation that he has established. And it means not only acceptance but also a willingness to engage in good works within that arrangement. When a Christian accepts this divine order and does God's work in it, he is living by faith.

What are the main features of Clement's idea of faith? One of his most striking statements occurs in chapter 32, verse 4:

> So we too, called through his will in Christ Jesus, are not justified through ourselves, or our wisdom, understanding, piety, or even works performed in holiness of heart, but through faith. Through this, the Almighty God has justified them all from eternity (32:4).

Here is a clear denial of justification by works in a manner that is reminiscent of Paul in Galatians 2:16:

> Knowing that a man is not justified from the works of the law but through faith in Jesus Christ. And we have believed on Christ Jesus that we may be justified through faith and not from works of the law because from works of the law no one will be justified.

Paul contrasts "works of the [Jewish] law" with faith, but Clement's contrast is even wider and more sweeping. If anything, Clement's denial of justification by works is more

---

2   1:2; 3:4; 5:6; 6:2; 10:7; 12:1,8; 22:1; 26:1; 27:3; 31:2; 32:4; 35:2; 42:5; 55:6; 58:2; 60:4; 62:2; 64:1. Most of these occurrences mean faith in the subjective sense (*fides qua creditur*), but some could be understood as the faith in an objective sense (*fides quae creditur*) such as 22:1.

3   "believe" (*pisteuo*) occurs in a theological sense of faith in 12:7; 34:4; 42:4; and possibly 42:3. The verb has non-theological meanings in 39:4 and 43:1.

emphatic than Paul's. Clement not only contrasts faith with "works of the law" as Paul does, but with "ourselves, or our wisdom, understanding, piety, or even works performed in holiness of heart." Religious acts and attitudes do not justify in Clement's view. Yet, as we shall see, faith is a forceful motivator to goodness and a holy life. Clement's view of faith involves the denial that moral and spiritual goodness in the Christian life originates from within the person. All goodness, righteousness, and holiness are a gift from God. Yet once that gift of faith is received, it shows itself by a life of goodness, righteousness, and holiness.

Faith for Clement is not a static concept; it is dynamic. Faith engenders other qualities, such as confidence in God's goodness and providence. In chapter 26, verse 1, Clement connects the phrase "in the confidence of good faith" with holiness. The genitive "of good faith" appears to be a genitive of origin, which suggests that good faith in a person generates confidence. Such confidence (*pepoithesis*) occurs again in the list of wonderful truths in chapter 35: "Beloved, how blessed and marvelous are the gifts of God! There is life in immortality, splendor in justice, truth in boldness, faith in confident affirmation, self-control in holiness" (35:1-2). All these magnificent blessings proceed from God as gifts. And therein is the key to understanding Clement's sense of the complete gratuity of grace and faith. All these gifts listed in 35:2 come as the free gifts of God. At the same time, faith can grow and take on other virtues as well, much as Peter says in 2 Peter 1:5, "[A]dd to your faith virtue, to virtue knowledge, to knowledge self-control, to self-control endurance, to endurance piety, to piety brotherly love, to brotherly love *agape*." The same process of growth in faith seems to lie behind Paul's triad of "faith, hope, and love" in 1 Cor 13:13: "Now faith, hope, and love abide. These three but the greatest is love."

The deep abiding connection between faith and hope or confidence is expressed by Clement in 58:2, where "the faith and hope of the elect" is identified as being the trinitarian God himself: "For God lives and our Lord Jesus Christ lives and the Holy Spirit [lives], the faith and hope of the elect." Because faith grows in a dynamic manner, it needs to be fired up, as Clement expresses in chapter 27.[4] In this way, the Christian becomes "perfect in faith" as Esther was (see 55:6). So, for Clement, faith is a state of life which engenders the godly qualities which characterize a Christian.

Recall the situation that Clement was facing in Corinth. He is addressing sedition, rebellion, and chaos in the church. What was needed to restore unity and peace within the church? One answer has to do with faith. Clement linked faith to obedience and to good order in the church. Faith provides clarity of vision, by which right may be distinguished from wrong. In chapter 3, verse 4, Clement constructs a causal moral sequence. When the fear of God is abandoned, then faith is obscured and moral disorder sets in, resulting in "each walk[ing] according to the desires of his own evil heart." When chaos reigns in the church, there is a complete loss of "justice and peace" (3:4).

In chapter 62, Clement pairs faith and repentance in a long list of positive attributes that should characterize the church and the individual Christian:

> We have handled every topic having to do with faith, conversion, authentic love, self-control, discretion, and perseverance, recalling that you should be completely pleasing to the Almighty God in righteousness, truth, and longsuffering. You should be united in love and peace, forgetting evil [done against you] with earnest forbearance, just as our forefathers, shown earlier, humbly did the things pleasing to the Father, the Creator God, and to all men (62:2).

The word I have translated as "conversion" is *metanoia*, the normal word in the New Testament for repentance. There, as here in Clement, *metanoia* means a change of heart and mind. It signifies a complete turn-around. In this letter, *metanoia*

---

4   "Let faith in him be rekindled within us, and let us consider that all things are near him" (27:3).

implies a reversal of attitudes toward the ordained leaders (presbyters) of the church. Since having faith in Christ means following the ordained order, which Clement so lavishly illustrates with examples drawn from the Old Testament, it also requires the personal characteristics listed in 62:2, that is, "conversion, authentic love, self-control, discretion, and perseverance." Without these accompanying virtues, faith means nothing.

What then is the end or *telos* of faith? In Clement, faith holds out the promise of a reward. In chapter 5, where Clement recounts the glorious martyrdoms of Peter and Paul, he speaks of Paul as having "received the noble renown [*kleos*] of his faith" (5:6). This renown comes as a reward for his being "imprisoned seven times, banished, and stoned." As Paul preached in the East and the West, his apostolic labors were rewarded with good fame as a herald of the gospel. This language recalls Paul's in 2 Tim 4:7-8:

> I have fought the good fight, I have finished the race, I have kept the faith. Finally, there is a crown of justice laid up for me with which the Lord, the just judge, will reward me on that day. And not only to me but to all who have loved his appearing.

Similar language is used by Clement in chapter 6, when he speaks of the heroic women, Danaids and Dircae. The athletic metaphor returns as "the race of faith" when Clement says that the women "attained to the sure course of faith and, though weak in body, they received a noble reward" (6:2). Like Paul, Clement sees perseverance in faith as being rewarded by God.

Faith and Works in Paul, James, and Clement

I would now like to triangulate Clement, Paul, and James to see whether their doctrines of faith are reconcilable. One method to accomplish this is to compare their respective treatments of Abraham's life, the father of faith. Unlike Paul and James, who invoke the life of Abraham to address the question of justification head on, Clement discusses the patriarch's life for other purposes. Clement first introduces Old Testament figures in chapter 4, with his recounting the story of Cain and Abel. Other examples of such figures are designed to show the destructive effects of jealousy and hate (see 4:8ff), the same underlying jealousy that threatens Christians in Corinth and Rome. When he introduces Abraham in chapter 10, Clement emphasizes a life of faithful obedience that was shown in his faith and hospitality. Clement cites Genesis 15:6, as Paul (Rom 4:3,9,22; Gal. 3:6) and James (Jas 2:23) do: "Abraham believed God, and it was counted to him as righteousness" (*ClCor* 6:6). Like Paul, Clement seems to link this being accounted righteous to the promise of a son and heir. Yet, for Clement, faith is intimately connected to the gracious act of receiving visitors:

> And again he says, "God led Abraham out and said to him, Look up at the sky and count the stars. If you can count them, your seed will be like them. Abraham believed God, and it was counted to him as righteousness." Because of his faith and his hospitality a son was given him in his old age, and through obedience he offered to God a sacrifice at one of the mountains he showed him (10:6-7).

In chapter 10, Clement treats Abraham from the standpoint of multiple events and stages of his life. Like James, Clement draws on the Jewish tradition that honored Abraham with the title "friend of God" (cf. Jas 2:23). And like the author of Hebrews 11, Clement interprets the visit of the guests in Genesis 18 and the sacrifice of Isaac in Genesis 22 as demonstrating essential parts of faith. Whereas Paul emphasized the temporal priority of Abraham's being justified before being circumcised (cf. Gen 15:6; Rom 4:10-11), Clement sees all of Abraham's actions as guided by and dependent on faith. Like James, Clement appeals to both Abraham's and Rahab's acts of hospitality as acts of faith. Why would Abraham's receiving the visitors (cf. Gen 18:1ff) and Rahab's reception of the spies (Josh 2:1ff) be accounted as faith? Because both involve receiving the divine message and presence.

Faith means clinging "to his blessing" and looking to "the ways in which he blesses" (31:1). One key to understanding Clement, then, is his summary statement in 31:2 as to why God blessed Abraham. Verse 31:2 asks, "For what reason was our father, Abraham, blessed? Was it not because he practiced justice and truth through faith?" Abraham could not have practiced justice (*dikaiosune*) and truth (*aletheia*) had he not lived by faith (*diapisteos*). So it seems that for Clement, while faith and works are not identical, neither can they be separated.

I have no doubt that the differences between the audiences to which Paul, James, and Clement were writing can account for the differences in their use of phraseology and tone. Though their phraseology differs, the substance of their teachings is similar and complementary, not contradictory. In Galatians, Paul was facing the problem of the Judaizers, who were attempting to force Gentile converts to undergo circumcision and to take on the whole Mosaic law as a precondition to their salvation (Gal 5:2). His argument in Galatians required a distinction between faith and works in such a way that the gratuity of justification is highlighted. Similarly, in Romans, Paul was addressing a church he had not yet visited. His overriding purpose was to explain the gospel he preached and which he wanted to proclaim in Spain (Rom 15:24-28). Paul's Letter to the Romans was in part intended to gather support for his Spanish mission from the Roman church, which at the very least had gained some prominence simply by virtue of its being in the center of the empire.[5] He therefore needed to explain his method as the apostle to the Gentiles. The message to the Gentiles was one of God's mercy in freely justifying the nations by faith. In the era of the new covenant, no longer was adherence to Judaism required. The God of the Jews was now also the God of the Gentiles by faith. And faith in this context

---

5   Rom 15:24: "Whenever I go to Spain, I hope to see you while passing through and to be sent on by you (*propempo*)." Some English versions soften *propempo*, by translating it "be helped," but the verb suggests that Paul wanted the Roman church to be one of his sending churches.

meant having the same trust in God as Abraham did. It meant a faith that worked itself out in love (Gal 5:6) and displayed a moral life (Gal 5:16-26), centered on the law of love (Rom 12:9-10; 13:8-10), but it did not mean living like Jews who still followed the Mosaic law. In Paul, faith is not opposed to works in faith but opposed to human works without God.

James faced a very different situation from Paul's. He addressed Christians who were attempting to use faith as a way of justifying their lack of good works. Faith was enough, his interlocutors said. If others wanted to go the way of works, that was fine, but they should not insist on everyone doing good works. Paul's audience confused faith and works, but James's made faith and works opposed. Both Paul and James distinguished clearly between faith and works, but both equally insisted that they cannot be separated as well. In light of the confusion made by the Judaizers, Paul had to emphasize faith as trust, faith as belief, faith as a response to grace. In response to a kind of fideism denying the value of action, James had to emphasize the inevitable and unbroken union of faith and works.

The situation in Corinth facing Clement was not the same as Paul's or James's. His need was not to stress faith and works per se but how to bring faith and works to bear on the sedition and rebellion against legitimate authority. Genuine faith generates virtue and submits itself to proper authority. The great biblical figures in the Old Testament stand as memorials to pursuing a life of faith that is lived out in action. Paul, James, and Clement do not teach the same things about faith and works, but neither do they contradict one another. They are complementary.

Faith and Virtue in Clement

Clement's view of Christian morality is much richer than the above discussion suggests. For Clement, as for the fathers of the church who followed him, humility was a root virtue, without which there was little hope of spiritual progress. In the context of his advice to the Corinthians, humility stands over against a rebellious spirit, in which someone seeks to challenge legitimate authority. In chapter 12, Clement recounts the story of Rahab and the Israelite spies whom the king of Jericho wished to kill. Rahab's virtue resided in her acknowledgement of the true God and his salvation. It was her submission to the instructions of the spies that saved her and her family. Clement draws this lesson from the story: "So let us be humbled, casting away all pride, blindness, foolishness, and wrath" (13:1). Humility submits to legitimate authority, while pride and arrogance pretend to know better. The Corinthians' rebellion against their presbyters arises from pride and can only be healed by true humility. The relevance of Clement's exhortations is obvious to anyone who sees members of the Christian faith today arrogantly asserting their superior knowledge over those legitimately established to guide the people of God. Ancient exhortations rarely lose their force because human nature is the same now as then.

For Clement, living by faith means imitation of Christ in his humility and of the saints who displayed a Christlike disposition. When Clement urges imitation of the Old Testament saints in these words, "Let us become imitators of those who walked around in the goat and sheep skins as they proclaimed the coming of Christ" (17:1), he is doing so after having recounted the humility of Christ taken from the words of Isaiah chapter 53. Bracketing his lengthy quotation in chapter 16 is his focus on the humility of Christ:

> Christ is for those of a humble mind, not those who raise themselves over his flock. The scepter of God's majesty, the Lord Jesus Christ, did not come with vaunting ambition or arrogance, though he could have, but [he came] with humility, as the Holy Spirit spoke of him…. See, O beloved, what model has been given to us! If the Lord humiliated himself in this way, what shall we do who have come through him under the yoke of his grace? (16:1-2,17).

The greatness and generosity of Jesus Christ lies in the contrast between what he is in himself (i.e., the scepter of God's majesty), and the path he chose. That path was to be an object of disgrace, rejection, hatred, and brutality, as the quotation from Isaiah 53 so vividly portrays. So, we might retranslate 16:1 thus: "Christ belongs only to those who are humble, not to those who exalt themselves over the flock." The call or vocation to the ordained ministry is never a matter of self-exaltation; and when it comes, it must be received with humility. Clement could have easily quoted Mark 10:45, where Jesus says, "The Son of Man did not come to be served but to serve and to give his life as a ransom for many" and urged the Corinthians to follow Christ's example of humility. But the exhortation to humility in 16:17 seems to be alluding to Matthew 11, by speaking of following Christ as coming under "the yoke of his grace." The text in Matthew can illuminate how "the yoke of grace" functions.

> Come to me, all who labor and are overburdened, and I will give you rest. Take my yoke on you and learn from me for I am meek and humble in heart. And you will find rest for your souls. For my yoke is good and my burden is light (Mt 11:28-30).

This text and Clement's allusion to it evokes the realization that it is Christ's humility which provides his disciples with the model of service and grace. Contrary to the expected burden and weight of a yoke, Christ's teachings seem light and liberating but only to those who are humble. The humility of self-denial that is directed to the good of others is living by faith.

So what does faith mean in Clement's *Letter to the Corinthians*? It means trust in the good promises of God, but it also means acting on those promises and cooperating with God's plan of salvation, just as Abraham and Rahab did. With the dire situation in the church at Corinth, faith means accepting the church order ordained by God. As Abraham acted on God's promises in faith, so the Corinthians are urged to submit in faith humbly to their leaders. Faith is the fount and source of all virtue, the greatest of which for Clement is humility.

CHAPTER SIX

The *Didache*: History and Literature

I n 1873, the Greek Orthodox Metropolitan of Nicomedia, Philotheos Bryennios, was rummaging through a library in Constantinople when he came upon a codex that caught his eye. The ancient book known as the Jerusalem Codex (*Codex Hierosolymitanus*) contained, among others, a short document that seemed to reflect other writings known from ancient times but which had never been found in one place. The Orthodox bishop sensed the importance of what he was looking at and began to read the Greek text carefully. As he surveyed the contents of this short treatise, he realized that he was looking at a copy of the lost work known as *The Teaching of the Twelve Apostles*, or the *Didache*. The world of early Christian scholarship in his day was scintillated beyond recognition by the publication of the *Didache* in 1883. Since that time, the amount of scholarship devoted to the *Didache* sometimes seems to be out of proportion to the short length of the document.[1] However, the reason for such attention has to do with its early date and what it reveals about Christianity in the late first or early second century. Many modern scholars believe that its importance lies in the fact that it occupies an

---

1   The *Didache* consists of 2,323 words.

intermediate place between the New Testament and the apostolic fathers.[2]

The *Didache* in the Ancient Church

A large part of the excitement modern scholars sensed was due to the fact that the *Didache* was known and used in the ancient church. In the first three centuries, some authors cited or referred to it as if it were part of the scriptural canon. And even if it were never accepted as scriptural in most places, it was still widely known and valued as a marker of the apostolic tradition. Later in the fourth century, when the canon of the New Testament was being more precisely defined, doubts were raised about whether the *Didache* originated from the apostles.

In the second century, Theophilus of Antioch quoted the negative form of the golden rule when he said, "Whatever a man would not wish to be done to himself, he should not do to another."[3] Comparing this with *Didache* 1:2 ("Everything that you wish not to be done to you, don't do to another"), we see how they differ from the positive form found in the New Testament (cf. Mt 7:12; Lk 6:31).[4] If the *Didache* originated in Syria, as many scholars think, Theophilus may have had access to it in Antioch, since that ancient city had both Syriac-speaking and Greek-speaking Christians. Also in the second century, Justin Martyr has definite affinities of language with the first chapter of the *Didache*, for Justin speaks of those following the Christian way as being patient and suffering injury for the sake of Christ.[5]

---

2   So believes one of the most prominent scholars of the *Didache* in the twentieth century, Willy Rordorf, in the Sources Chrétiennes edition published originally in 1978 and reissued in 1998. We simply do not know what individual or community composed the *Didache*. For the sake of convenience, I will refer regularly to the writer as "the Didachist," but this is only a convention for the sake of presentation.

3   *Autolycus* bk. 2 ch. 34.

4   In the Deuterocanonicals, Tobit 4:15 reads, "What you hate, do not do to anyone."

5   *First Apology*, 1.16. Some scholars have argued that Justin is not so much using the *Didache* as the Gospel of Matthew, which the Didachist seems to use as well.

A third witness from the late second century is Clement of Alexandria, whose *Stromata* is citing *Didache* 3:5 ("My child, do not become a liar, for lying leads to stealing") where he quotes it as if it were Scripture.[6]

We encounter mention of the *Didache* in the early fourth century when Eusebius lists it among the writings that are not genuine (i.e., not in the canon of the New Testament), "among those spurious writings should be ordered these: *The Acts of Paul, The Shepherd [of Hermes], The Apocalypse of Peter, The Epistle of Barnabas,* and the one called *The Teachings of the Apostles.*"[7] To understand Eusebius in his proper context, it is important to note his distinction between recognized, disputed, and non-genuine writings, with the *Didache* being in the last category. What this indicates, of course, is that these writings, while being rejected from the canon of the New Testament, were nevertheless highly valued among many in the ancient church. That the *Didache* continued to be important in the fourth century is seen in Athanasius's *Festal Letter 39*, in which he says that the work was read in the church (of Alexandria) for the instruction of the faithful while being excluded from the biblical canon.[8] Even though there are allusions to the *Didache* after the fourth century, historical references began to trail off. Its recovery had to wait until 1873.

The *Didache*: One or Many?

Almost all historical questions about the *Didache* depend on the question of the unity of the document. Is it the work of one author who wrote it in a fairly short period of time, or is

---

6   "It is such a one that is by Scripture called a 'thief.' It is therefore said, 'Son, be not a liar; for falsehood leads to theft.' " *Stromata* bk. 1 ch. 20. Rordorf discusses other possible references to the *Didache* in Clement. See Rordorf, p. 125.

7   *Ecclesiastical History* bk. 3 ch. 25.

8   "But for greater exactness I add this also, writing of necessity; that there are other books besides these not indeed included in the Canon, but appointed by the Fathers to be read by those who newly join us, and who wish for instruction in the word of godliness ... and that which is called the Teaching of the Apostles, and the Shepherd." Athanasius *Festal Letter* 39.

it a compilation of different documents patched together by some unknown editor? At first glance, the latter seems to be the case. For a document of a little over two thousand words, the *Didache* contains several disparate sections that have little connection to one another:

	SECTIONS OF THE *DIDACHE*
1.	The Ways of Life and Death Section (ch. 1-5). Chapters 1 to 4 expound the way of life, and chapter 5 the way of death. Chapter 6 is a transitional passage.
2.	The Liturgical Section (ch. 7-10) deals with baptism (ch. 7), prayer (ch. 8), and the liturgy of the Eucharist (ch. 9,10).
3.	The Church Order Section (ch. 11-15).
4.	The Section on the Final Things (eschatology; ch. 16).

The first section (ch. 1-5), contrasting the ways of life and death, is modeled on many biblical precedents, including those Jesus himself gives in the Sermon on the Mount (Mt 5-7). These in turn are based on examples in the Old Testament. For example, many scholars have noted that Psalm 1 stands at the head of the Psalter precisely to say that the praises of Israel in the Psalter promote the way of righteousness in contrast to the way of unrighteousness. We know that late Judaism before and after Jesus's time had many extensions of the Hebrew tradition of contrasts between good and evil. So too, the Didachist piles on moral exhortations in a short span in order to delineate what it means to be a follower of the Way. It is here that the Didachist shows his probable dependence on the Gospel of Matthew.

The second section (ch. 7-10) is devoted to liturgical matters, specifying how baptism and the Eucharist should be performed, as well as giving regulations for prayer and fasting. The liturgical section was particularly astonishing to modern scholars because it revealed how early Christians were worshiping in a manner that no other document from the ancient church had ever done, not even documents in the New Testament. Here are prayers connected to the Eucharist that seem to be the roots of later liturgies long known. Here too is found (ch. 8) the Lord's Prayer (Our Father) that almost exactly matches the form in the Gospel of Matthew. The *Didache* is the earliest document showing how the church assimilated Jesus's prayer into its life.

The third section on questions of church order is the only one that is problematic. The others seem relatively self-contained. The third section, however, gives instruction on how to deal with visiting apostles, prophets, and teachers. These wandering ministers had apparently raised the question as to how one would know the true from the false. The Didachist gives a number of tests by which one could know how to handle these itinerant preachers. It is also here that chapter 14 seems out of place; it would seem better to have it go with the second section (ch. 7-10). Yet, if the testing of the itinerant apostles and prophets was to take place in a liturgical context, the mentioning of the Lord's Day in chapter 14 would fit in to some degree. Chapter 15 gives instruction about choosing bishops and deacons. While some of these concerns in this third section seem unrelated, they all seem to have to do with proper order in the church.

The fourth and final section (ch. 16) contains exhortations to vigilance and readiness for the *parousia* (second coming) of Christ. It suggests that the process of sanctification must continue toward perfection until the arrival of the last day (*eschaton*). And like many passages in the New Testament, this section warns of the increase of evil, hate, and lawlessness in the last days.

Many scholars (e.g., Rordorf) see these distinct sections as coming from once-separate sources that have been put together by an unknown redactor (editor). Others (e.g., Milavec) have noted that the whole document does contain transitional elements, such as chapter 6, such that the *Didache* could be read as a unified document. That precise question will probably never be resolved, but it does cause the modern reader to pay close attention to the content of each section and the transitions between them. The unity of the document is a matter of attending carefully to its internal clues, but there are external connections as well.

The *Didache* and the Gospel of Matthew

It is natural that scholars attempted to find agreements and disagreements between the *Didache* and other early Christian documents, especially those in the New Testament. For many years, there was an assumed dependence on the Gospel of Matthew, but in the latter part of the twentieth century this hypothesis was rejected by a significant number of scholars. Some have plausibly argued that the *Didache* and Matthew's Gospel represent independent manifestations of a common Christian tradition.[9] Most of the affinities between Matthew and the *Didache* are in the Two Ways section of the treatise, and we have many other instances of such teaching in other documents, both Jewish and Christian. For example, *The Epistle of Barnabas* has a section treating the Two Ways similar to that found in chapters 1 to 5 of the *Didache*. It may be that the teaching on the Two Ways circulated in many forms, two of which are found in the *Didache* and the Sermon on the Mount in Matthew.

But given our purposes here, it would be most helpful to note some of the similarities between Matthew's Gospel and the *Didache*. They almost all occur in the Two Ways section:

Di 1:2:	Everything that you wish not to be done to you, don't do to another.
Mt 7:12:	Everything that you wish that others do to you, do also to them.
Di 1:3:	[B]less those who curse you and pray for your enemies.
Mt 5:44:	Love your enemies and pray for your persecutors.
Di 1:4:	If someone gives you a slap on the right cheek, turn the other to him and you will be perfect.

9   A few scholars have argued that Matthew was dependent on the *Didache*. For a fuller discussion, see Milavec, pp. 693-739.

Mt 5:39:	If someone slaps you on the cheek, turn to him the other.
Di 1:4:	If someone presses you into service for one mile, go with him for two.
Mt 5:41:	Whoever presses you into service for one mile, go with him two.
Di 1:4:	If someone takes away your garment, give him your tunic as well.
Mt 5:40:	If someone wishes to sue you for your tunic, give him your garment as well.
Di 1:5:	If someone takes from you what is yours, don't demand it back.
Mt 5:42:	Give to him who asks and do not turn away from the one who wishes to borrow.
Di 3:1-2:	Do not be prone to anger for anger leads to murder. Don't be a jealous, quarreling, or violent person. From all these are born murders
Mt 5:21-22:	Everyone angry with his brother will be liable to the judgment.
Di 3:7:	But be meek for the meek will inherit the earth.
Mt 5:5:	Blessed are the meek for they will inherit the earth [land].
Di 4:12:	You should hate all hypocrisy and everything that does not please the Lord.
Di 8:1:	Do not practice fasting with the hypocrites.
Mt 6:1ff (e.g., v. 2):	When you give alms, do not blow a trumpet as the hypocrites do.

All the above parallels, of course, find other reverberations in the New Testament, but there does seem to be a noticeable similarity between the Sermon on the Mount in Matthew's Gospel and the form of these commands in the *Didache*. However, the most extensive parallel is between the form of the Lord's Prayer in *Didache* 8:2 and the form in Matthew 6:9-13.[10]

---

10   For some of the minor differences, see my commentary on 8:2 of the *Didache*.

Didache 8:2	Matthew 6:9-13	Luke 11:2-4
Our Father, who are in heaven.	Our Father in heaven.	Father
Hallowed be your name.	Hallowed be your name.	Hallowed be your name.
Your kingdom come.	Your kingdom come.	Your kingdom come.
Your will be done on earth as it is in heaven.	Your will be done on earth as it is in heaven.	
Give us today our daily bread.	Give us today our daily bread.	Give us each day our daily bread.
Forgive us our debt as we forgive our debtors.	Forgive us our debts as we also have forgiven our debtors.	And forgive us our sins for we ourselves forgive everyone indebted to us.
Lead us not into temptation but deliver us from evil.	Do not bring us into temptation but deliver us from the evil.	And do not bring us into temptation.
For yours is the power and glory forever. Pray this three times a day.		

In the original Greek text of each prayer, none of the versions agrees with another in every respect, but Matthew's version has a greater similarity to that of the *Didache* than to Luke's version. Here are some of the obvious differences:

1. The *Didache* and Matthew have "Our Father" and "in heaven," while Luke has simply "Father."

2. The *Didache* and Matthew have the petition "Your will be done on earth as it is in heaven," which Luke omits.

3. The *Didache* and Matthew have the word "today" (*semeron*), while Luke uses a phrase "each day" (*kath hemeran*).

4. The *Didache* and Matthew use the word "debt," while Luke uses "sins."

5. The *Didache* and Matthew use "as we also," while Luke uses "for we ourselves."

6. The *Didache* and Matthew include the petition "deliver us from evil," while Luke omits it.

While there are some minor differences between the *Didache's* and Matthew's versions, the similarities suggest that the Didachist took his form of the Our Father from the Gospel of Matthew or that the communities behind the respective texts inherited a common tradition. In any case, there is no doubt that the version from Matthew and the *Didache* became the standard in time. There is, however, a second similarity worth noting. The context of the Didachist quoting the Lord's Prayer is clearly liturgical or a context of public prayer. Matthew's Gospel also places the same prayer in the context of public prayer. In Matthew 6:1-8, Jesus contrasts the ostentatious nature of Jewish prayers with his own advice. And while he does advise entering into one's closet (v. 6), this is meant more as a metaphor for entering into true communion through prayer than physical residence. The context of public prayer is shared by both authors. Luke, however, sets the prayer in a context of private instruction when the disciples ask Jesus to teach them to pray (Lk 11:1). This private prayer seems to reflect the Jewish custom of rabbis teaching their disciples a fixed prayer which would identify them as his disciples. Both contexts are important, but it would have made more sense to the Didachist to use Matthew's version. As references to the New Testament in my commentary make evident, the teaching of the Didachist is a reflection and extension of the biblical authors.

The Date of the *Didache*

The discovery of the *Didache* is a fascinating story for those who appreciate the art of historical writing. When any such document is found, it opens up new possibilities for understanding ancient Christianity. Like many documents from antiquity, scholars have proposed a variety of dates for the *Didache*. Most date it in the range from ca. A.D. 50 to 150, although some have put it later. The document itself gives us no sure indicators as to when it was written, and so students of the *Didache* must infer its date from the actual theological and liturgical content of the document. This involves comparing its teachings with other known documents, both in the New Testament and in the early centuries. When dating an ancient Christian document like the *Didache*, the best that can often be achieved is to establish a beginning (*terminus a quo*) and an ending date (*terminus ad quem*), but even then this process is complicated by the uncertainty associated with other documents.

Two salient facts seem to suggest a date between ca. 50 to 150. On the later end, the *terminus ad quem*, Justin Martyr's and Clement of Alexandria's use of the *Didache*, suggest that it may well have been an accepted Christian document by about 150. We think that Justin was writing around the mid-second century. We know that Clement was writing in the last quarter of the second century. Given that Clement especially treats the *Didache* as being at least close to possessing scriptural authority, it is likely that our document was written well before he was writing in Alexandria. On the other end, as for the *terminus a quo*, the *Didache's* sure affinities with and possible use of the Gospel of Matthew suggest that it originates from the late first century. Scholars like Rordorf, who believe that the Didachist did not use Matthew but shared a common oral tradition with it, may be willing to date it even earlier, say around A.D. 50. Comparisons of this kind have led almost all students of the *Didache* to the conclusion that we have here one of the earliest witnesses to Christianity outside the New Testament itself.

The discovery and publication of the *Didache* was a monumental event in the nineteenth century, and reading it today has lost none of its force. Even with many historical and literary questions unresolved, the modern reader may glean much from the document that still shapes theology today. Most of all, it affords Christians today a unique look at the beliefs and practices of some of their earliest forebears.

CHAPTER SEVEN

The Theology of the *Didache*

Earlier I said that the excitement surrounding the discovery of the *Didache* had to do with its contents and what they reveal about early Christianity. What exactly does the *Didache* teach? I will not be able to treat every topic here but will concentrate on two that stand front and center in the mind of Christians: the church and the Eucharist.[1]

The Church in the *Didache*

The word *ekklesia* (church) occurs four times in the text of the *Didache* (4:14; 9:4; 10:5; 11:11). Two of these (9:4; 10:5) are in the liturgical section, and their meaning and associations are not difficult to discern, but a look at their context reveals something illuminating about the Didachist's doctrine of the church.

> As the broken bread was scattered on the mountains and then gathered into one, thus let your church be gathered from the ends of the earth into your kingdom because yours is the glory and the power through Jesus Christ forever (9:4).

---

1   Given the enormous amount of scholarship on the *Didache*, the reader is encouraged to examine the bibliographies of the authors cited in these footnotes. The most extensive is that of Milavec.

> Remember, Lord, your church, to rescue it from every evil and
> to make it perfect in your love, and from the four winds gather
> it completely sanctified into your kingdom which you have
> prepared (10:5).

The first quote, 9:4, is a clear plea for unity in the church,
but it is a unity of an eschatological kind, that is, one that will
only be complete in the final kingdom of God. The association with the broken bread (*klasma*) is not only an analogy
based on natural things, it also signifies that the ministry of
the church through its preaching of the gospel and the celebration of the Eucharist is aimed at the unity of all humanity.
The plea for unity in the context of celebrating the Eucharist
represents the church's deepest longing for the unity of all. The
liturgical celebration of the church is both a thanksgiving —
the root meaning of *eucharistia* — and an urgent cry for the
completion of God's plan of gathering all into the one body.
Such a plea grows naturally out of Paul's teaching on the connection between the Eucharist and unity, "Since there is one
bread, we many are one body for we all partake of the one
bread" (1 Cor 10:17) and that of Ignatius of Antioch in his
Letter to the Ephesians, when he speaks of "breaking one bread
which is the medicine of immortality" (20:2). We know from
later liturgies of the church that the petition for unity in the
church has always been a part of its worship. The discovery of
the *Didache* only revealed how early this idea was.

There are, however, threats to the unity of the church, and
so the liturgical prayer of the *Didache* says, "rescue it from every evil and to make it perfect in your love" (10:5). Pleas for
the protection of the church are needed because the threats
are multiple. In the *Didache*, there are few indications of a
threat against the community from the pagan world around
it, unlike, say, the *Martyrdom of Polycarp*. Most of the threats
arise from *within* the church, broadly defined. First, there is
the threat of false prophets and teachers envisioned in the
third section (ch. 11-14) who are charlatans and opportunists.
Second, there is the threat of unworthy bishops and deacons,

which is why the moral qualifications for the offices are spelled out in chapter 15. Third, there is always the threat of internal discord, which is why the Didachist urges fraternal reconciliation in 14:2 and correction in 15:3. Finally, the threat of moral dissolution is always present, which makes sense of the Ways of Life and Death Section in chapters 1 to 5.

In asking God to "rescue [the church] from every evil and make it perfect it in your love," the community is asking God to fulfill within them the command to love their enemies in 1:3. In keeping with Jesus's teaching in the Sermon on the Mount, the Didachist wants Christians to go beyond justice and live by the law of love. This love is what will lead to perfection. In 16:2, the believers are reminded, to "gather frequently and seek those things appropriate for your souls. For the whole time [allotted] for your faith will not profit you unless you are perfected in the final moment." The church's worship is envisioned as a means for this needed perfection. The most striking truth behind these pleas for unity in 9:4 and 10:5 is that they show how from the very beginning the church valued unity and realized at the same time how imperfect its corporate life was.

The last instance of *ekklesia*, which is also relevant to our understanding of the church, is more enigmatic and has evoked different translations and interpretation. I have translated the phrase in 11:11 as follows: "Every true prophet, who has been approved, in performing the mystery of the church in this world but not teaching to do what he does, will not be judged by you. His judgment lies with God, for the ancient prophets did likewise." The phrase in question that has caused so much discussion is "in performing the mystery of the church in this world" (*eis musterion kosmikon ekklesias*). Unlike some interpretative problems where the translation is not in doubt, this phrase in 11:11 cannot be understood apart from a particular translation. Here is a sample of possible translations:

Holmes: "who does something with a view to portraying in a worldly manner the symbolic meaning of the church"

Kirsopp-Lake: "though he enact a worldly mystery of the church"

Ehrman: "who acts on behalf of the earthly mystery of the church"

Milavec: "doing a worldly mystery of the church"

Rordorf: "who acts in view of the mystery of the church in the world"[2]

Quacquarelli: "who acts for the earthly mystery of the church"[3]

One question has to do with the meaning of *musterion* here. Does it mean simply a "secret"? Or is the presence of the church a mystery in a general sense, which the outside world cannot understand? Or does *musterion* here have the sense of "sacrament" as the word undeniably came to mean later? A second question has to do with the exact meaning of the words "of the church" (*ekklesias*). The third has to do with the precise meaning of the preposition *eis*. All the translations ("with a view to," "on behalf of," "for") cited above are possible, but treating the prepositional phrase as if it were a direct object (Lake, Milavec, mine) is possible too.

Whatever the exact syntax of the construction, I offer here an interpretation consistent with the general sense of the passage and with the *Didache* as a whole. Taking the phrase "of the church" (*ekklesias*) as standing in apposition,[4] we could retranslate the phrase "performing (or doing) the mystery in the world, that is, the church" or possibly "acting with a view to the mystery in the world, that is, the church." On this reading, the church is seen as a mysterious presence in the world — God's secret, if you will — but not in a purely symbolic sense, at least not in the modern sense of symbolic. Thus, Holmes's

---

2   Rordorf's French is "qui agit en vue du mystère de l'église dans le monde."

3   Quacquarelli's Italian is "che agisce per il mistero terreno della Chiesa."

4   Technically called an "explicative genitive."

translation of *musterion* as "symbolic meaning" fails to grasp all that the phrase implies. I favor Rordorf's and Ehrman's translations, where *musterion kosmikon* is taken as indicating the place where the mystery is enacted. What is that mystery that is performed or enacted? It is the reality of the church's presence in the world. The meaning and significance of the church is supramundane; it originates in and is fed by a heavenly life from beyond this world. Yet, the church exists in the world and so must exist as a mystery whose meaning the outside world cannot grasp. The prophet mentioned in verse 11 is tried and true as he acts in behalf of or with a view to the mysterious character of the church. Even if his teaching fails to live up to the proper standard, the community is not to judge him. His judgment lies with God.

Lastly, in the occurrence of *ekklesia* found in 4:14, the Didachist urges his readers to confess their transgressions in church and where the word seems to retain more of its original sense of "assembly." When the church gathers for worship, the worshipers are to have a pure conscience, a point reiterated in chapter 14, "On the Lord's Day, once you have gathered, break the bread [of the Lord], and celebrate the Eucharist, after having confessed your transgressions that your sacrifice may be pure" (14:1).

These four instances of the word "church" (*ekklesia*), taken together, indicate that the Didachist sees the church as a reality in this world, whose life and meaning originate from beyond this world. The church in the world is always on the path toward perfection, and the dangers facing the church are not insignificant. Thus, as the church gathers for worship, its members must seek a purity of heart made possible through the confession of sin. Realizing its all-too-imperfect state, the church must pray for the greater realization of its final end, the unity of all its members.

The Eucharist in the *Didache*

If the church is the mystery of God in the world (11:11), the central reason for this lies in its eucharistic liturgy. The *Didache* is so important for our understanding of early Christianity because of what it reveals about the worship of the church at this incipient stage of the church's history.[5] Here the word group of *eucharistia* is used in a way that seems innovative on the surface but comports well with Ignatius of Antioch's use and the mid-second-century writings of Justin Martyr.[6] Even if we translate the verb *eucharisteo* in chapters 9 and 10 as "give thanks," the noun is almost certainly being used as a proper noun (Eucharist) rather than as a common noun (thanksgiving). The Didachist clearly uses the noun as an already accepted term for their liturgy in (9:1,5).[7]

Rordorf has pointed to several expressions in the liturgical prayers that indicate that the church is founded on Israel's messianic vocation.[8] The church is conceived of as fulfilling the messianic vocation of the great servant of God, David, and his heir, Jesus Christ. According to 9:2, Christ has made known the true meaning of "the holy vine of David." By implication, the church is called to the same vocation. In the Old Testament, the vine imagery is used of Israel (Ps 80:8-19; Is 5:1-7). Isaiah 5:7 identifies the vine(yard) of the Lord as the house of Israel. This forms the background for Jesus's speaking of himself as "the true vine" (Jn 15:1). Jesus is *the* great son of Israel who will fulfill the vocation which Israel failed to fulfill.

---

5   There has been a vigorous debate over whether the liturgical prayers in chapters 9 to 10 are eucharistic properly speaking or an agape feast, with scholars arguing strongly on one side or the other. See the discussions in Rordorf, pp. 38-48. If we step back and ask which hypothesis fits the evidence of later texts (e.g., Justin Martyr), the answer clearly falls on the side of the eucharistic interpretation. The *Didache* reflects the foundation of this tradition.

6   The NT never uses the word *eucharistia* as a designation for the liturgy or the sacrament of the "the Lord's Supper," as Paul called it.

7   "Concerning the Eucharist, celebrate the Eucharist in this way" (9:1), and "Let no one eat or drink from your Eucharist except those who are baptized in the name of the Lord" (9:5).

8   Rordorf, pp. 45-46.

And so the holy vine of God in the Old Testament, the people of Israel, was summed up in its greatest king, David. The Son of David now comes as the one who accomplishes Israel's vocation. The church then takes up the mission of Christ and fulfills the same mission. Temple imagery is also applied to the church in 10:2: "We thank you, Holy Father, for your holy name, which you have made to dwell in our hearts, and for the knowledge, faith, and immortality which you made known to us through Jesus your child." This placing of the name on the heart is an allusion to the temple where the name of God resides. In Deuteronomy, we find the promise that God will choose a place for his name to dwell (e.g., Deut 12:5). Later, this promise is realized in the building of the temple under Solomon.

So, the eucharistic prayers of chapters 9 and 10 have a two-fold function. They *reflect* the church's self-understanding, but they also *reinforce* that understanding. The self-conception of the church in the *Didache*, as in many liturgies later, focuses on the Person of Jesus Christ. Jesus, like David, is the servant (*pais*) of God. He is one through whom God receives glory and power. Jesus is the revealer of "knowledge, faith, and immortality" (10:2) and the one who gives "spiritual food and drink and eternal life" (10:3). This last phrase from 10:3 is worthy of closer examination. The full verse reads:

> You, Lord Almighty, have created all things for your name's sake. You have given food and drink to men for enjoyment that they may thank you. But you have graciously given us spiritual food and drink and eternal life through your child [Jesus] (10:3).

The parallel between natural and spiritual food is evident:

A. You have given food and drink to men for enjoyment that they may thank you.

B. You have graciously given us spiritual food and drink and eternal life through your child [Jesus].

The differences are significant too. The author uses two verbs for "give." In line A, it is *didomi*, the simple verb "to give." In line B, however, he uses *charizomai*, "to give graciously." The second verb is appropriate for the higher gift, since it is a result, not of nature, but of grace. The natural food and drink meant in line A results in human enjoyment, whereas the spiritual food and drink in line B results in eternal life. The addition of "through your child [Jesus]" indicates that this second kind of food is salvific and therefore of a heavenly origin. Though the writer does not use the language employed by Paul of "the body and blood of Christ," 10:3 suggests that the food and drink of the Eucharist was considered more than natural food, in fact, the conveyor of eternal life.

The Eucharist as Sacrifice in the *Didache*

What is even more striking about the Didachist's language is its association with the notion of sacrifice. In 14:3, the Didachist quotes from Malachi 1:11 and 14 in connection with the confession of sin in Christian worship. Chapter 14 of the *Didache* contains two moral exhortations: one to confess one's sins "that your sacrifice my be pure" (14:1) and the other to reconcile with one's neighbor "that your sacrifice not be defiled" (14:2):

> On the Lord's Day, once you have gathered, break the bread [of the Lord], and celebrate the Eucharist, after having confessed your transgressions that your sacrifice may be pure. Let no one who has a quarrel with his friend join you until they reconcile, that your sacrifice not be defiled. This is what was said by the Lord, "In every place and time offer to me a pure sacrifice because I am a great king, says the Lord, and my name is marvelous among the Gentiles" (14:1-3).

The exhortations of verses 1 and 2 are reminiscent of Jesus's exhortation in Matthew 5:23-24: "If you offer your gift on the altar and there remember that your brother has something against you, leave your gift there before the altar and go, first be reconciled to your brother. Then come offer your gift." Both

Matthew and the Didachist speak of a context of worship. Both imply that the purity of the gift offered is related to the purity of the intention of the worshiper. However, the Didachist ties confession and reconciliation to the purity of the sacrifice by quoting a text which is never quoted in the New Testament, Malachi 1:11,14.[9]

The form of the Greek text in the *Didache* does not match that of the Septuagint, which follows closely the original Hebrew. The latter in the Massoretic Text reads:

> For from the rising of the sun to its setting my name is great among the nations [Gentiles]. In every place incense is offered to my name and a pure gift [sacrifice] for my name is great among the nations [Gentiles], says the Lord of Hosts (1:11).

> For I am a great king, says the Lord of Hosts, and my name is awe-inspiring among the nations [Gentiles] (1:14b).

In the Septuagint, these verses read:

> For from the rising of the sun to its setting my name is glorified among the nations [Gentiles]. In every place incense is offered to my name and a pure sacrifice for my name is great among the nations [Gentiles], says the Lord of Almighty (1:11).

> For I am a great king, says the Lord Almighty, and my name is awe-inspiring among the nations [Gentiles] (1:14b).

Carefully compare these with the version in the *Didache*: "In every place and time offer to me a pure sacrifice because I am a great king, says the Lord, and my name is marvelous among the Gentiles" (14:3).

Clearly the Didachist has lifted a phrase out of verse 14 ("I am a great king") and inserted it into his quotation from verse 11. Perhaps most striking is that our author adds the word "time" to the Malachi text. Both the Hebrew and the Septuagint of Malachi 1:11 have "in every place," but the Didachist has "In every place and time." This relates to the overall impact of the meaning, but only if we appreciate the Malachi text in a

---

9 Some have found an allusion to Mal 1:11 in Rev 15:4, but the parallel is opaque at best.

Jewish milieu. For any Jew, whether in Malachi's day or later, to acknowledge that the Gentiles can offer an acceptable sacrifice to the Lord would have been shocking. The only true sacrifices acceptable to God are those performed in the temple in Jerusalem. Yet here is the prophet asserting (or predicting) that the pagans will offer "a pure sacrifice" to God.

If we take the Didachist as an early expression of something undeniable in later writers, then the reason that he quotes this text has to do with its associations with the Eucharist. In the mid-second century, Justin Martyr quotes the same verse in his *Dialogue with Trypho the Jew*:

> Therefore, God speaks about those sacrifices which were at one time offered by you all, as I said, through Malachi, one of the twelve prophets. My will is not among you, says the Lord, and I will not accept the sacrifices from your hands. Therefore, from the rising of the sun to its setting my name is glorified among the Gentiles, and in every place incense and a pure offering is offered to my name because my name is great among the nations, says the Lord, but you defile it.

> Now he speaks beforehand about the sacrifices offered by us Gentiles in every place — that is the bread of the Eucharist and similarly the cup of the Eucharist — when he says that we glorify his name, but you defile it.[10]

Later Justin quotes from Malachi 1:11 again when he stresses that the Eucharist is the sacrifice that is acceptable to God because Jesus Christ is the new and final high priest.[11]

So, what is the "pure sacrifice" that is "offered in every time and place?" The Didachist does not say explicitly, but, given that he says this in a context of worship, it is reasonable to understand him as making an allusion to the Eucharist. Since the writer applies Malachi 1:11 to the matter of reconciliation between Christians, it is also reasonable to see the notion of sacrifice latent in the text, for it is a sacrifice which reconciles Christian to Christian and ultimately both to God. The purity

---

10   *Dialogue with Trypho the Jew* ch. 41 sec. 2-3.

11   Ibid., ch. 116,117.

of the sacrifice is related to the purity of heart that is implied in the reconciliation, but that personal purity is possible because the sacrifice is none other than Christ himself. And this conclusion is strengthened by the Didachist's addition of the word "time" to the Malachi quotation. He wishes to emphasize that the sacrifice of Christians in the Eucharist is celebrated constantly throughout the earth.

Even though the *Didache* is a relatively short document (2,323 words), its topics, phraseology, and structure have provided a rich resource for our understanding of what the early church believed. The two topics presented here are only a smattering of its depth and breadth. The excitement that accompanied its discovery in 1873 is not diminished by time. It stands as a unique window into the life and faith of the earliest Christians after the apostles.

CHAPTER EIGHT

Clement of Rome's
Letter to the Corinthians

SALUTATION

The church of God on its pilgrimage[1] in Rome [writes] to the church of God on its pilgrimage in Corinth, to those called, sanctified in the will of God through our Lord Jesus Christ. Grace and peace be multiplied[2] to you from God Almighty through Jesus Christ.

CHAPTER 1

(1) Because of the sudden and repeated misfortunes and experiences that have happened[3] to us we think we have more

---

1   "pilgrimage" represents *paroikeo*, "to sojourn," and is used of resident aliens rather than citizens, for which the normal Greek is *katoikeo*. The author implies that both the Roman and Corinthian Christians are citizens of a different country (the kingdom of heaven). See 1 Pet 1:1 and 2:11, and especially Heb 11:13-16.

2   "multiplied." Clement indicates here, as did the apostle Peter his teacher (cf. in 1 Pet 1:2 and 2 Pet 1:2), the desire for an abundance of blessings for the recipients of the letter.

3   Clement's mention of misfortune and calamities may be a reference to the persecutions experienced by Christians in Rome during the reign of Domitian, when this letter was penned. Domitian was emperor from A.D. 81 to 96. If Clement's attention to the troubles of his own church had preoccupied him, the delay in writing to the church in Corinth would be understandable. Still, it indicates that bishops in the early church saw the scope of their pastoral ministries as extending beyond their own diocese.

slowly turned our attention to those matters that are sources of strife among you, beloved, that is, of this unholy and profane rebellion so foreign and alien to God's elect. Some reckless and rash people have kindled this sedition with such a loss of sense that your name, so solemn, well-known, and loved by all, has been greatly blasphemed.[4] (2) For who, when they visited you, did not approve your faith, so firm and full of virtue? Who could fail to be amazed at your wise and gentle piety in Christ? Who did not proclaim the magnificence of your hospitality and not bless your perfect and secure knowledge? (3) You have conducted yourselves in every way without favoritism, and you have walked in God's commands by being subject to your leaders and rendering fitting honor to the presbyters among you. You have enjoined the young to think on moderate and solemn things. The women you have commanded to conduct all their affairs in a blameless, devout, and pure conscience, each loving her own husband appropriately. You have taught them to work at home devoutly by the rule of submission, always acting wisely.

CHAPTER 2

(1) You all were of a humble mind without boasting, being submissive rather than dominating, giving gladly rather than receiving.[5] By being satisfied with Christ's provisions and by heeding his words, you embraced them in your inner hearts[6]

---

4 Some forty years after Paul addressed the same church about disunity (see 1 Cor 1:10ff), the Corinthian church again is besieged with sedition. In Paul's time, the problem was factionalism (see 1 Cor 1:10ff), whereas now it seems to be outright rebellion against properly ordained leaders (clergy). Clement here follows Paul's teaching in Ephesians 4:1-6, that unity is an essential attribute of the church. Rebellion leads to disunity. See chapter 2 above, in the introductory essays.

5 Clement's words reflect Jesus's as recorded in Acts 20:35. See also chapter 13, where Clement develops this and related themes.

6 *tois splagchnois*, lit., "bowels" — a biblical word to denote the deepest seat of the affections. Paul uses it in Phil 1:8 ("I long for you with the bowels of Christ Jesus") and in Col 3:12 ("Clothe yourselves ... with bowels of compassion."). Clement praises his hearers for allowing the word of Christ to dwell richly in their hearts (see Col 3:16).

with his sufferings before your eyes.[7] (2) In this way, a deep and rich peace was given to all and an insatiable desire to do good as well.[8] And a full outpouring of the Holy Spirit came upon all.[9] (3) And [being] full of holy counsel with good intention, with devout confidence extend your hands to God Almighty, asking for his mercy in case you sinned unwillingly.[10] (4) There was a struggle day and night for the brotherhood,[11] so that the number of his elect may be saved with mercy and conscience.[12] (5) Sincere and blameless you were and forgiving[13] in dealing with one another. (6) All disorder and schism were abominable to you. You mourned the transgressions of your neighbors. You judged their failures to be your own. (7) You were unchangeable in doing good, "ready for every good work."[14] (8) Being adorned with all virtuous and venerable conduct,[15] you accomplished everything out of reverence for him. The commands and requirements of the Lord have been written on the tablets of your heart.

---

7 Paul has a similar idea in Gal 3:1: "O foolish Galatians, who has bewitched you before whose eyes Jesus Christ was portrayed as crucified."

8 The city of Corinth was infamous for its immorality. So, to say that the Christians there had "an *insatiable* desire to do good" was a high commendation.

9 Cf. Rom 5:5: "the love of God has been poured out in our hearts through the Holy Spirit who was given to us."

10 "unwillingly" (*akontes*) means sinning without forethought and malice. It means an inadvertent fall into sin. The opposite is mortal sin, as expressed in Heb 10:26: "If we willingly keep on sinning after receiving the knowledge of the truth, there no longer remains a sacrifice for sin."

11 Like the bishops who are concerned for the whole church, every Christian should make it his goal to help others to salvation by his struggles. Instead of "a struggle … for the brotherhood," Kleist translates this as "vied with one another," which suggests a struggle against one another. All other English translations agree with mine.

12 "with mercy and conscience." Some MSS have "fear" or "dread" instead of "mercy," which is what Ehrman chose as the reading. But "fear" only occurs in one MS, while "mercy" occurs in all the others. A later scribe probably changed it because using "mercy" and "conscience" together seems out of place in this context. Clement probably means that the elect will be saved through Christians exercising mercy and maintaining a clear conscience in the midst of their struggles.

13 "forgiving" (*amnesikakoi*) is translated by others as "without malice."

14 See Eph 2:10.

15 *politeia* means conduct as a citizen in society.

CHAPTER 3

(1) All honor and expansion[16] were given to you, and what was written has been fulfilled, "The beloved ate, drank, became fat, were fattened, and kicked back."[17] (2) From this come jealousy and envy, strife and sedition, persecution and instability, war and slavery.[18] (3) Thus, the dishonorable rose up against the honorable, the inglorious against the glorious, the foolish against the wise, the young against the elders. (4) For this reason, justice and peace are absent, in that each one abandons the fear of God and becomes dim-sighted in faith, does not walk in his lawful commands nor conducts himself in accord with the custom of Christ, but each walks according to the desires of his evil heart, taking in unrighteous and godless jealousy through which "death came into the world."[19]

CHAPTER 4

(1) Thus it is written,[20] "It happened that after some days Cain brought some fruits of the ground as a sacrifice to God and Abel brought one from the firstborn of the sheep and of their fat portions. (2) And God looked on Abel, but on Cain and his sacrifices he did not pay heed. (3) And Cain was very sad and his countenance fell. (4) God said to Cain, Why have you become so sorrowful and why is your countenance so

---

16 *platusmos* has been variously translated as "scope" (Kleist), "growth" (Holmes), and "opportunity for expansion" (Grant). Clement probably means that the Corinthian church has enjoyed considerable growth from the time of the apostles.

17 This is a conflated quotation from the Septuagint version of Deut 32:14-15. This text says that Jeshurun (Jacob) forsook God because of his prosperity. Clement makes the same charge against the Corinthian church.

18 The church in Corinth has experienced division and strife as a result of its prosperity, a common theme in Scripture. The church of Laodicea boasted of its wealth but was destitute in spiritual riches (Rev 3:14-22).

19 A quotation from Wis 2:24, "by the envy of the devil death entered the world." This text has also influenced Paul in Rom 5:12, "As sin entered world through one man, and death through sin, and in this way death passed through to all men …"

20 The following is a quotation from Gen 4:3-8 from the LXX version, from which Clement always quotes. He probably did not know Hebrew. There are several differences between the Greek (LXX) version and the Hebrew text that we now have (MT), as noted in the following comments.

fallen? If you bring an offering correctly but you do not divide correctly,[21] have you not sinned? (5) Be calm. Its [sin's] return is to you and you will rule it. (6) And Cain said to his brother Abel, "Let us go into the field. And it happened that while they were in the field Cain rose up against Abel his brother and killed him." (7) See, brothers, how jealousy and envy brought about fratricide. (8) Because of jealousy, our father, Jacob, escaped from the presence of his brother Esau.[22] (9) Jealousy made Joseph be persecuted until death and delivered him into slavery.[23] (10) Jealousy forced Moses to flee from Pharaoh's presence, the king of Egypt, when he heard from his fellow countryman, "Who appointed you ruler and judge over us? Do you want to kill me as you killed the Egyptian yesterday?"[24] (11) Because of jealousy Aaron and Miriam lodged outside the camp.[25] (12) Jealousy led Dathan and Abiram to Hades while alive because they rebelled against Moses, the servant of God. (13) Because of jealousy, David experienced envy not only from foreign peoples but was persecuted by Saul, the king of Israel.[26]

CHAPTER 5

(1) But let us cease from ancient examples and come to those athletes nearest [to our time]. Let us take the noble examples of our generation. (2) Because of jealousy and envy, the greatest and most righteous pillars were persecuted and attained to death. (3) Let us place before our view the good

---

21 It is not clear what this dividing means. Perhaps it means that Cain did not give the best part of his sacrifice to God, whereas Abel did. The entire sentence, "If you bring an offering correctly but you do not divide correctly, have you not sinned? Be calm" is not in the MT. Either the LXX was translating from a different Hebrew text or is giving a highly interpretative translation.

22 See Gen 27:41ff.

23 See Gen ch. 37.

24 See Ex 2:14.

25 See Num ch. 12, esp. vv. 13-15.

26 See the stories of David and Saul in 1 Samuel ch. 18,19.

apostles. (4) Let us take Peter,[27] who, because of unjust jealousy, endured not one or two but many hardships. Once he gave his testimony, he went to the place of glory owed him. (5) Because of jealousy and strife, Paul showed forth a prize of endurance. (6) Being imprisoned seven times, banished, and stoned, he became a herald in the East and the West and received the noble renown of his faith. (7) Having taught the whole world righteousness and arrived at the farthest boundaries of the West, he gave his testimony before rulers; so he exchanged this world and arrived at the holy place, after he became a great example of endurance.[28]

CHAPTER 6

(1) A great multitude of the elect were joined to these men who lived holy, worthy lives.[29] Once these suffered many outrages and torments because of jealousy they became the most beautiful[30] example among us. (2) Because of jealousy, the women Danaids and Dircae[31] were persecuted and suf-

---

27   It is no accident that Clement chose Peter and Paul as his examples of endurance and martyrdom. Early on, Peter and Paul were viewed as the co-founders of the church of Rome. Irenaeus, the late-second-century bishop of Lyons, has a long passage in which he recounts Peter and Paul as pillars of the Roman church. See *Against Heresies* bk. 3 ch. 3 sec. 2-3. It should not be forgotten that Irenaeus in his youth knew Polycarp of Smyrna personally. The latter, as bishop of Smyrna, knew Ignatius of Antioch, who probably knew Peter personally. Thus there seems to be a direct line from Peter through Ignatius and Polycarp to Irenaeus. Still today, the church of Rome celebrates the co-founding of the church there by Peter and Paul on June 29 of every year.

28   Endurance is a key virtue that leads to final salvation. Mt 10:22 and 24:13 say, "He who endures to the end will be saved." Jas 1:3 states, "the trial of your faith produces endurance." Peter and Paul were both exemplars of endurance in faith.

29   Clement uses the verb *politeuomai*, which means "to live as a free citizen." Either he means that these men (e.g., Peter and Paul) lived as citizens of the kingdom of God, or they lived in the Roman empire as holy citizens even though the Roman pagans may not have acknowledged it. The main point of chapter 6 is that jealousy has destroyed the lives of the faithful too, including women, marriages, and even great cities.

30   Most English translators have chosen "illustrious." I have chosen "beautiful" because the idea of aesthetic honor lies behind the Greek word *kalliston*. The beauty of their Christian witness lies in inverse proportion to the "outrages and torments" they experienced at the hands of pagan officials.

31   "the women Danaids and Dircae." These words have long evoked perplexity on

fered terrible and lawless torments. Thereby they attained to the sure course of faith and, though weak in body,[32] they received a noble reward. (3) Jealousy alienated wives from their husbands and altered what was said by our father Adam, "this is bone of our bones and flesh of our flesh."[33] (4) Jealousy and strife overturned great cities and uprooted great nations.

CHAPTER 7

(1) Beloved, we are not only commanding you with an admonition but also to remind ourselves. We are in the same arena and the same contest is set for us.[34] (2) So, let us leave the empty and futile ways of thought and come to the famous and pious rule of our tradition.[35] (3) Let us observe what is beautiful and pleasing and acceptable in the sight of him who made us. (4) Let us fix our sights on the blood of Christ and know how precious it is to his Father. Because having shed it

the part of commentators. Some have thought that these are the names of actual Christian women martyred in the reign of Nero, perhaps after the great fire of Rome that began 19 July A.D. 64 and burned for six days. Others have seen them as comparing the courage of martyred Christian women to the stories of heroic women. The story of Dircae is appropriate. She was tied to a bull by her hair and dragged along in the amphitheater. Still others have suggested that the text was corrupted in transmission early on. Lightfoot and Quacquarelli accept an emendation which then would read, "young maidens and female slaves" instead of the proper names. No historical solution seems definitive but the general point is clear. The hatred and venom of pagan persecutors did not spare even women, who were thought to be weaker because of their lesser bodily strength.

32 *hai astheneis to somati* is literally "weak in body." Grant translates "despite their physical weakness." Kleist's rendering ("in spite of the weakness of their sex") is less literal but does capture the point of Clement's using these women as examples. He is commending their courage, something which in the ancient world was thought to be the preserve of men.

33 Gen 2:23.

34 By the time Clement was writing this letter in the mid-90s, the famous Roman Coliseum had been completed, though it underwent modifications during Domitian's reign. When Clement therefore speaks of "an arena," he may very well have been thinking of the same structure visible today in Rome.

35 *paradosis* is the normal word for "tradition" in the NT. Of the thirteen occurrences, Paul uses the word in a positive sense three times (1 Cor 11:2; 2 Thess 2:15; 3:6). The tradition refers to some aspect of apostolic teaching that was passed on in written or verbal form (see 2 Thess 2:15). Clearly, Clement sees this tradition as the foundation of the church.

for our salvation, he brought the grace of repentance to the whole world.[36] (5) Let us proceed through all the generations and learn that the Master has given a place of repentance for those who desire to turn to him. (6) Noah preached repentance and those who obeyed were saved. (7) Jonah proclaimed destruction to the Ninevites. Those who repented of their sins propitiated[37] God by seeking [him] and receiving salvation although they were strangers from God.

CHAPTER 8

(1) The ministers of God's grace spoke about repentance through the Holy Spirit.[38] (2) And the Lord of all himself spoke about repentance with an oath, "For, as I live, says the Lord, I do not desire the death of the sinner, as much as repentance."[39] He added this good token, (3) "Repent, O house of Israel, from your lawlessness. Say to the children of my people, even if your sins rise from earth to heaven and they are redder than scarlet and blacker than sackcloth, and if you turn to me with your whole heart and say, 'Father,' I will hear you as holy people."[40]

---

36   The expression "the blood of Christ" or similar locutions occurs in the NT in 1 Cor 10:16; 11:27; Heb 9:14; 10:19; 1 Pet 1:2; 1:19; and 1 Jn 1:7. It is never used with a verb of seeing such as here. *Atenizein* means "to stare, to gaze, to fix one's eyes." Clement explicitly says that this blood was shed for the world's salvation. Why does he use a verb of vision with the blood of Christ? Perhaps he is alluding to a practice of elevating the cup of the blood of Christ. If so, this would be the earliest mention of such a practice in the history of Christianity.

37   To propitiate God means to satisfy the demands of divine justice. Almost all religions have an idea of appeasing God through sacrifice. Clement sees in the case of the Ninevites and Jonah a mention of biblical appeasement. It is not through animal sacrifice but through a broken and contrite spirit that God's justice is met. See Ps 51:17.

38   It is not clear whether Clement is saying that repentance is through the Holy Spirit or that the speaking of the servants of God is through the Spirit.

39   This is a paraphrase of Ez 33:11. *Metanoia* is the word in the NT and here for "repentance" or "conversion." Etymologically, it means a change of mind or heart. In the LXX, *metanoia* usually translates the Hebrew word *shub*, which means "turning around" as it does in Ez 33:11. Like the NT authors, Clement sees conversion or repentance as essential for the Christian as it was for the people of Israel.

40   This last sentence could be translated, "I will listen to you as a holy people should." Clement seems to be quoting from the OT, but his wording does not correspond to any one text. It appears to be an amalgam of many texts, including Is 1:18-20.

(4) And in another text he says it this way, "wash yourselves and become clean. Remove evil from your souls in my presence.[41] Cease from your evil [ways], learn to do good. Seek judgment.[42] Rescue the one who has been mistreated. Do justice for the orphan and vindicate the widow and come, let us reason, says the Lord, though your sins are red like crimson, I will whiten them like snow. And even if they are red, I will whiten them like wool. If you are willing to obey me, you will eat the good things of the earth. If you are not willing to obey me, the sword will devour you. For the mouth of the Lord has spoken these things."[43] (5) So wanting all his beloved to partake of repentance, he confirmed it by his all-powerful will.

CHAPTER 9

(1) Therefore, let us obey his magnificent and glorious will. As we beg for his mercy and goodness,[44] let us fall down and turn to his compassion, abandoning futile effort, strife, and jealousy leading to death.[45] (2) Let us fix our gaze on those who have served his magnificent will so completely.[46] (3) Let us take Enoch, who by being found righteous in obedience, was translated and death did not find him.[47] (4) Noah, be-

---

41 Lit., "before my eyes."

42 Presumably in the sense of justice.

43 Is 1:16-20.

44 Many translators choose "goodness" for *chrestotes* (e.g., Holmes, Jaubert), while others choose "kindness" (e.g., Ehrman) or "lovingkindness" (e.g., Kleist). *Chrestotes* has a broad meaning of God's gentle disposition toward his creatures.

45 In this verse, Clement combines human and divine actions in short compass. Christians must turn away from futile strife and jealousy with obedience to God's will, while acknowledging that only God's mercy and goodness provide the strength for their actions.

46 As Clement begins to recount those in the history of salvation who have served God well, he probably implies that the presbyters of Corinth, against whom the church is rebelling, are among those who have served well and therefore do not deserve the opposition they are receiving.

47 Gen 5:24 and Heb 11:5. Enoch is the first in the list of examples of faithful obedience going through chapter 12 (Noah, Abraham, Lot, Rahab). Clement is following the examples of Heb 11, where the biblical author stresses the faith of the ancient patriarchs. In both the NT and in Clement, we can observe how faith was always linked to obedient actions. See the commentary on 10:6.

ing found faithful through his service, preached restoration[48] to the world, and through him the Master rescued the living creatures that entered the ark in harmony.[49]

CHAPTER 10

(1) Abraham, who was called a friend of God, was found faithful in being obedient to the words of God. (2) Through obedience he left his homeland, his relations, and his father's house so that he might inherit the promises of God by leaving behind his small country, weak family ties, and insignificant house. For he [the Lord] said to him, (3) "Go out from your land, your relatives, and your father's house to the land that I will show you. And I will make you into a great nation, and I will bless you and make your name great and you will be blessed. I will bless those who bless you and I will curse those who curse you, and in you all the tribes of the earth will be blessed."[50] (4) And again, when he separated from Lot, God said to him, "Lift up your eyes and look from the place where you are now to the north, the south, the east, and the west because all the land you see I will give to you and your seed forever. (5) I will make your seed as the dust of the land. If you can count the dust of the land, your seed can be numbered as well."[51] (6) And again he says, "God led Abraham out and said to him, Look up at the sky and count the stars. If you can count them, your seed will be like them. Abraham believed God, and it was counted to him as righteousness."[52] (7) Because of his

---

48   The Greek word *paliggenesia* denotes a renewal or rebirth of the world. It was used by the Stoics to speak about the rebirth of the universe after the great conflagration. The same word is used in Mt 19:28, where it denotes the rebirth of the world at the end of time. Baptism gives the Christian the beginning or down payment on that world to come. See Tit 3:5, where it speaks of "the washing of rebirth," a phrase that all the church fathers refer to baptism.

49   Some translate *en homonoia* as "peacefully" and others as "in harmony" or "in concord." Clement implicitly gives a command for Christians to act harmoniously as did the simple beasts in Noah's day.

50   Gen 12:1-3.

51   Gen 13:14-16.

52   Gen 15:5-6.

faith and his hospitality[53] a son was given him in his old age, and through obedience he offered to God a sacrifice at one of the mountains he showed him.[54]

CHAPTER 11

(1) Lot was saved from Sodom because of hospitality and godliness as the whole country was judged with fire and brimstone. While the Lord showed clearly that he will not abandon those who trust in him, he placed those who were not so inclined under punishment and terror. (2) His wife, who came out with him and who thought differently and was not in agreement, became a sign so that she became a salt pillar to this day that all may know that those who are double-minded[55] and hesitate with regard to God's power for judgment become a sign[56] for all generations.

CHAPTER 12

(1) Rahab the harlot was saved because of her faith and hospitality. (2) When the spies were sent out by Joshua, the son of Nun, to Jericho, the king of the land knew that they had come to spy out his land, and he sent out men to arrest them, so that, after arresting them, they might put them to death. (3) So, when the hospitable Rahab received them, she hid them

---

53   The mention of hospitality may seem strange to modern ears, but Clement commends the hospitality of Abraham, Lot, and Rahab to emphasize that this was the way they demonstrated their faith. Clement may be thinking of the visitors coming to Abraham in Gen 18:1-15.

54   Clement combines a quotation from Gen 15:5-6, about Abraham believing God, with the narrative in Gen 22, about his sacrifice of Isaac. These are the same chapters on which Paul and James comment in different ways. See chapter 5 in the introductory essays above for a discussion of faith, works, and sanctification in Paul, James, and Clement.

55   "double-minded" translates *dipsuchos*, a word used in Jas 1:8: "a double-minded man, unstable in all his ways." James says this of the man who asks God for wisdom but who doubts that God is good enough to grant it. Clement applies the same idea to a person who turns back from God's call, as did Lot's wife.

56   In this verse, Clement uses two different words for "sign." The first (*semeion*) is the standard term used in the NT, while the second (*semeiosis*) meant more of an inference from a sign in the classical period. Here Clement seems to use them interchangeably or nearly so.

on the upper level under the flax. (4) Those appointed by the king said, "It was to you that the spies of our land came. Bring them out; the king commands it." But she answered, "The men you are seeking came to me all right, but immediately they left and went out into the road." She pointed them in the opposite direction. (5) And she said to the men, "I know for sure that the Lord God is delivering this land to you for fear and dread has fallen on its inhabitants. So when you happen to take it, save me and my father's house." (6) And they said to her, "So it will be as you have said. So, when you know that we are near, gather all your people under your roof, and they will be preserved for as many as are outside the house will die."[57] (7) They gave her a sign that she might hang a scarlet cord outside her house, making clear that redemption will come about through the Lord's blood for all who believe and hope in God.[58] (8) See, brethren, that not only faith but prophecy[59] was evident in this woman.

CHAPTER 13

(1) So let us be humble, casting away all pride, blindness, foolishness, and wrath. Let us do what is written.[60] For the Holy Spirit says, "Let not the wise man boast in his wisdom or the mighty man in his strength, nor the rich man in his

---

57   Clement recounts the story of Rahab and the spies that is in Joshua chapter 2, but he does not quote the LXX text. He may have retold the story from memory.

58   The color symbolism of the scarlet cord as a sign for the blood of Christ began to be used very early by Christians and has persisted to this day. Justin Martyr is even more explicit than Clement: "God proclaimed beforehand the salvation that would come to the human race through the blood of Christ. There was also the symbol of the scarlet cord which the spies sent by Joshua son of Nun to Jericho gave to Rahab the harlot. This symbol signifies the blood of Christ." *Dialogue with Trypho* 111, 3-4. Heb 9:19 mentions scarlet wool and may have been a suggestive source for this tradition.

59   Clement uses the term "prophecy" here in the broad sense of anything that is a sign of future truths. Rahab herself was such a sign of faith, as the NT authors assert (see Heb 11:30-31 and Jas 2:25), and the scarlet cloth is as well.

60   Jaubert rightly emphasizes the connection between chapter 12 about Rahab and the exhortations of chapter 13. Rahab was saved by her submission to the spies' command to hang the scarlet cloth outside her house. She becomes an example of humility.

riches but let him who boasts boast in the Lord, to seek him and to perform judgment and righteousness."[61] Especially [we should] recall the words of the Lord Jesus that he said when teaching gentleness and patience. (2) Thus he said, "Be merciful that you may receive mercy. Forgive that you may be forgiven. As you do, it will be done to you. As you give, it will be given to you. As you judge, you will be judged. As you are kind, so kindness will be shown to you. The measure with which you measure, it will be measured to you."[62] (3) Let us confirm ourselves in this command and in those requirements so that those who are obedient may walk in his holy words with humility. For the holy message says, "On whom shall I look [with favor] except the one who is meek, and quiet, and who respects my words?"[63]

CHAPTER 14

(1) It is just and holy, brothers, that we become obedient to God rather than to follow those leaders in the pride and instability arising from a foul jealousy. (2) It is not an ordinary harm but a great danger to which we will be subject if we give ourselves over to the will of men who launch into strife and sedition to alienate us from the One who has our good in mind.[64] (3) Let us be kind to one another in the compassion and sweetness of the One who made us, (4) for it is written, "The inhabitants of the earth will be kind, and the guileless will be left on it but those who are lawless will be utterly destroyed from it."[65] (5) And again it says, "I saw the godless exalted and lifted up like the cedars of Lebanon. I passed by and

---

61 Clement quotes Jer 9:23 but modifies it in the same way that Paul does in 1 Cor 1:31 and 2 Cor 10:17.

62 These correlations about judgment and forgiveness are an expanded paraphrase of Lk 6:37-38 and Mt 7:1-2.

63 Is 66:2. The word for "quiet" (*hesuchia*) in the LXX translates the Hebrew "crippled in spirit." The Lord's love is for those who feel themselves unable to assert themselves.

64 Clement's strong condemnation of schism and sedition in the church reflects Paul's exhortations to unity to the Corinthians. See 1 Cor 1:10-17 and Phil 2:1-3.

65 See Prov 2:21-22 and Ps 37:9.

behold, he was not [there]. I sought out his place and I did not find it. Protect innocence and look at uprightness because there is a remnant for the peaceful man."[66]

CHAPTER 15

(1) So then, let us join ourselves to those who live in peace with holiness and not those who want peace in hypocrisy.[67] (2) He says somewhere, "This people honors me with their lips, but their heart is far from me."[68] (3) And again, "They bless with their mouth, but curse in their heart."[69] (4) Again he says, "They loved him with their mouth, but lied to him with their tongue. Their heart was not correct with him, nor were they committed to his covenant."[70] (5) "Therefore, let the deceitful lips that speak lawlessness against the righteous be silent."[71] And again, "May the Lord utterly destroy deceitful lips, a big talking tongue, those who said, 'We brag with our tongue. Our lips are ours. Who is the Lord over us?'[72] (6) I will raise [them] up from the wretchedness of the poor and from the groaning of the workers, says the Lord. I will grant them salvation. (7) I will speak openly to them."[73]

---

66   Clement's quotations from Ps 37:35-36 in this chapter liken the current rebels in the Corinthian church to the wicked of the OT. It demonstrates how serious is schism in the church because God intended the church, like ancient Israel, to be united.

67   Clement begins this chapter with the contrast between two ideas of Christian peace. One is connected with holiness (piety); the other pretends to want peace but without submission to the ordained structures of the church as God has established them. Peace without truth or justice is empty.

68   The original statement appears in Is 29:13, though Clement seems to be quoting from Mt 15:8 or Mk 7:6.

69   Ps 62:4.

70   Ps 78:36-37. The last phrase may also be translated, "nor were they entrusted with his covenant."

71   Ps 31:18.

72   The exact source of this quote is unclear. It may be an amalgam of several OT texts.

73   Ps 12:5.

CHAPTER 16

(1) Christ is for those of a humble mind, not those who raise themselves over his flock.[74] (2) The scepter[75] of God's majesty, the Lord Jesus Christ, did not come with vaunting ambition or arrogance, though he could have, but [he came] with humility, as the Holy Spirit spoke of him. For he said, (3) " 'Lord, who has believed our report and to whom has the arm of the Lord been revealed?' We proclaimed his coming, like a child, like a root thirsty in dry land. He had no form or glory; we saw him and he possessed no form or beauty. Rather his appearance was dishonorable, falling short of human form. [He was] a man of blows and toil, known to bear infirmity because his person[76] was rejected, dishonored, and not even counted [among men]. (4) He bears our sins and experiences anguish for us; we accounted him as being in toil, pain, and mistreatment. (5) He was wounded for our sins and was weakened for our lawless deeds. The punishment of our peace was on him; by his stripes we were healed. (6) We all like a sheep have gone astray, each one deceived by his own way. (7) The Lord delivered him up for our sins and he did not open his mouth because of the mistreatment. He was led away like a sheep for the slaughter. Like a lamb before its shearers he was silent, not opening his mouth. In this humiliation, his judgment was borne.[77] (8) Who will tell of his generation since his life was taken away from the earth? (9) He has come into death because of my people's lawless deeds. (10) And I will give evil

---

74   Clement here reflects the biblical and historic teaching that the call to ordained ministry does not come from one's own self but from humbly seeking to be a shepherd through God's call.

75   To speak of Christ as the "scepter of God" refers to his kingship, his power. But as Jesus himself said, "The Son of Man did not come to be served but to serve and to give his life a ransom for many" (Mk 10:45). Clement's quotation of the Suffering Servant Song in Is 53 points to Christ as the humiliated servant who rules by his willing submission to God's will.

76   Lit., "face." This is a Hebraism in which "face" is used for "person."

77   My translation of this last phrase fits the context well, but it could also be translated "justice was denied him in his humiliation," as Ehrman does.

ones in place of his tomb and the rich in place of his death[78] since he did no crime nor was any guile found in his mouth. And the Lord wishes to cleanse him from the wound. (11) If you give [something in exchange for] your sin, your soul will see a long-lived posterity. (12) And the Lord wishes to rescue his soul from distress, to show him light, and to form his understanding, to justify the righteous man as serving the many well. And he himself will bear their sins. (13) Therefore, he will inherit many [people] and will divide the spoils of the strong. This is the reason his soul was delivered over to death. And he was counted among the unlawful. (14) He bore the sins of many and was delivered up for their transgressions."[79] (15) Again he says, "I am a worm and not a man, the reproach of men and something people despise. (16) All who see me mock me, they speak with their lips, they shake their head. He hoped in the Lord; let him rescue him; let him save him since he desires him."[80] (17) See, O beloved, what model has been given to us! If the Lord humiliated himself in this way, what shall we do who have come through him under the yoke of his grace?[81]

CHAPTER 17

(1) Let us become imitators of those who walked around in the goat and sheep skins as they proclaimed the coming of Christ. And we speak of Elijah and Elisha, and even of Ezekiel, the prophets who have testified to these things. (2) A great witness was given about Abraham who was named a friend of God. And as he gazes at the glory of God, protracted on the

---

78 The first two clauses of this verse are difficult to translate. The LXX is probably mistranslating the Hebrew, and Clement is quoting the LXX. The meaning of the original Hebrew is probably, "He made his tomb with the wicked and with the rich in his death."

79 With a few minor variations, 16:3-14 is a quotation from the LXX version of Is 53:1-12.

80 Ps 22:6-8. This text also influenced the language of Mt 27:39; Mk 15:29; Lk 23:35.

81 "The yoke of his grace" is never found in the NT, but the idea is implied in Mt 11:28-30. Unlike the normal expectation of a yoke being a burden, "the yoke of grace," that is, the yoke Christ gives, places the Christian into service of a loving and kind Savior.

ground, he said, "I am dust and ashes."[82] (3) It was also written of Job, "Job was a just and blameless man, a true worshiper of God, abstaining from all evil."[83] (4) But he accuses himself, "No one is clean from a stain, nor is his life even of one day."[84] (5) Moses was called "faithful in all his house,"[85] and by his service God judged Egypt through scourgings and torture. He was honored greatly; he did not boast but spoke from the revelation at the bush, "Who am I that you would send me? I have a weak voice and am slow of speech."[86] (6) And again, "I am but a breath from a pot."[87]

CHAPTER 18[88]

(1) What should we say about David, testified to by God who said, "I found a man after my own heart, David the son of Jesse; in eternal mercy I have anointed him?"[89] (2) But he [David] also says to God, "Have mercy on me, O God, according to your great mercy, and according to the multitude of your compassions, wipe out my transgressions. (3) More and more wash me from my iniquity, and cleanse me from my sin because I know my iniquity and my sin is always before me. (4) Against you alone have I sinned, and done what is evil in your sight that you may be justified in your pronouncements and prevail in your judgment. (5) Behold, I was conceived in iniquity, and in sins did my mother give me birth. (6) Behold, you love truth. You have shown me the guileless and secret things

82 Gen 18:27.

83 Job 1:1.

84 This is a paraphrase of Job 14:4-5.

85 A commendation of Moses in Num 12:7 quoted also in Heb 3:2-5.

86 Clement combines Ex 3:11 and 4:10.

87 This quotation is not found in the OT or any known source.

88 Chapter 18 is almost entirely a quotation of Ps 51 (Ps 50 in the LXX). As in the other examples, Clement finds the greatest virtue of the OT saints in their humility. Psalm 51 is David's lament after he was confronted by Nathan the prophet, who pronounced God's judgment on David's double sin of adultery (with Bathsheba) and murder (of Uriah her husband). See also 2 Sam 12:1ff.

89 Clement's quotation appears to combine Acts 13:22, Ps 89:20, and 1 Sam 13:14.

of your wisdom. (7) You will sprinkle me with hyssop, and I will be clean. You will wash me and I will be whiter than snow. (8) You will make me hear gladness and rejoicing; my humiliated bones will exult. (9) Turn your face away from my sins and wipe out all my iniquities. (10) Create in me a clean heart, O God, and renew a right spirit in my inmost being. (11) Do not cast me away from your presence nor remove your Holy Spirit[90] from me. (12) Give to me the joy of your salvation and strengthen me with a guiding[91] spirit. (13) I will teach transgressors your ways, and the ungodly will return to you. (14) Rescue me from the guilt of shedding blood,[92] O God, God of my salvation. (15) My tongue will rejoice greatly [in] your justice. Lord, open my mouth and my lips will declare your praise. (16) Because if you desired sacrifice, I would give it. You did not delight in burnt offerings. (17) Sacrifice for God is a broken spirit, and God will not despise a broken and humbled heart."

CHAPTER 19

(1) Through the obedience, humility, and lowliness of so many and such great witnesses he not only made us better but also the generations before us, those who received the words of God in reverence and in truth. (2) Because we share in many great and glorious deeds, let us return to the goal of peace handed down to us from the beginning. And let us fix our gaze on the Father and Creator of the whole cosmos.[93] And

---

90   I have capitalized "Holy Spirit" because Christian writers such as Clement generally take this as referring to the third Person of the Trinity. The Hebrew text of Ps 51:11 could also be translated, "Don't take the spirit of holiness from me."

91   Hemmer translates *hegemonikos* as "a spirit of generosity" (*un esprit de generosité*, p. 43). But this adjective normally means "guiding or leading." I see no reason to depart from its standard meaning.

92   Lit., "from bloods," a Hebraism translated literally in the LXX. The Hebrew text of Ps 51:14 is referring to David's act of murdering Uriah the Hittite, the husband of Bathsheba.

93   I have chosen the English "cosmos" for the Greek cognate term (*kosmos*), which is normally translated as "world" in the NT. Here, however, Clement displays his awareness of the root meaning of the word, which is "an ordered whole." God's ordering of the universe becomes a pattern for human action, as can be seen in

let us join ourselves to the great and superabundant gifts and beneficence of peace.[94] (3) Let us see him in [our] mind and look unto his patient will with the eyes of the soul. Let us think seriously on how devoid of anger he is toward all his creation.

CHAPTER 20[95]

(1) The heavens are subject to him in peace as they roll along by his administration.[96] (2) Day and night finish the course ordered by him, in no way hindering one another. (3) Sun, moon, and the chorus of stars unfold the limits[97] appointed for them in harmony without any deviation according to his ordinance. (4) By his will, the earth like a pregnant woman[98] provides complete nourishment at the proper times for men, beasts, and all living animals without deviating or changing any of the decrees made by him.[99] (5) Untraceable [paths][100] of the abyss and ineffable judgments of the netherworld are con-

---

Clement's use of *atenizein*, meaning "to fix one's gaze." By looking intently at God, the Christian becomes peaceful and harmonious like God.

94   This sentence could be translated several ways, but the overall thought is clear. Christians should seek peace in the church by receiving God's gifts of peace. God's intention is for the church to reflect the harmony that is seen in the cosmos. This theme is developed further in chapter 20.

95   Chapter 20 is a hymn in praise of God's goodness in his creation and providential guidance of the cosmos. It reflects the OT idea of God's care for his creation as in Psalms 8 and 19. A similar expression of wonder at the orderliness of nature can be found in Stoic writers of the Hellenistic period. Cicero recounts some of these in *On the Nature of the Gods* (*De natura Deorum*) bk. 2 ch. 98-127.

96   Early Christian liturgies often incorporated praises to God for the creation such as *Apostolic Constitutions* 8, 12. Many scholars have seen here reflections of the early Roman liturgy, much like *ClCor* chapters 59 to 61, although others (e.g., Grant) deny it.

97   "unfold the limits" (boundaries) is a fairly literal translation that means the course of the seasons stay the course of their alternation.

98   Most translators smooth out Clement's metaphor by saying that "earth becomes fruitful." Though this is clearly the meaning of the sentence, I have retained the metaphor of pregnancy (*kuophoreo*) to emphasize that the earth is like a woman who gives her children food.

99   Notice that v. 4 has moved from the emphasis of the first three verses on the regularity and orderliness of the natural realm to the organic interdependence of the parts.

100 The word "paths" does not occur in the Greek text, but it seems to be implied, although others have translated this passage differently.

strained by the same commands. (6) The basin of the bound-less sea, having been combined in its workmanship into a col-lection, does not transgress the bars encircling it.[101] Rather, as he commanded it, so it does. (7) For he said, "Thus far shall you come, your waves will break in you."[102] (8) The ocean that is boundless for men and the worlds beyond it are set right by the same orders of the Master.[103] (9) The seasons of spring and summer, fall and winter, yield one to the other in peace. (10) The reservoir of winds completes their service at their proper seasons without hindrance. The ever-flowing streams, created for enjoyment and use, without fail furnish the breasts[104] for nourishment of human life. The least of the beasts make their mating in harmony and peace. (11) It is all these things that the great Creator and Master has fixed to exist in peace and harmony, showing kindness in them abundantly for us who have taken refuge in his mercies through our Lord Jesus Christ. (12) To him be glory and majesty forever and ever. Amen.

CHAPTER 21

(1) Be careful, beloved, lest his many benefits do not end up in judgment for us. This will happen if we live unworthily of him by failing to do what is good and pleasing in his sight with harmony.[105] (2) For somewhere he says, "The Spirit of the Lord is like a lamp that searches the depths of the heart."[106] (3) Let us see how near he is because nothing in our thoughts

101 The idea of boundaries in nature is found in Job 38:8-11.

102 Job 38:11; "in you" refers to the sea.

103 My translation follows Grant's interpretation that this verse refers to the Atlantic Ocean, while Jaubert cites ancient sources referring to the lost city of Atlantis under the sea. Some moderns falsely think that the ancients were unaware or uninterested in worlds beyond the scope of their travels.

104 Like the metaphor of pregnancy in v. 4, Clement here speaks of the earth in femi-nine terms of giving suck with its breasts. The evoked feelings of peace, love, and harmony are to be the model for life together in the church.

105 The word translated as "harmony" (*homonoia*) could also be rendered "unity of mind." Clement now emphasizes that our human lives must reflect the beauty and harmony of the natural world he recounted in chapter 20. This theme will be repeated many times in Christian history in science, philosophy, and theology.

106 A paraphrase of Prov 20:27.

and reasoning escapes his notice.[107] (4) For it is right that we not become deserters from his will.[108] (5) Rather than offend God, let us [be willing] to offend men who are foolish, ignorant, arrogant, and boastful in the pride of their speech. (6) It is the Lord Jesus Christ whose blood was shed for us that we should revere. Let us praise those who lead us; let us honor the presbyters; let us instruct the young with training in the fear of God; let us help our wives to embrace the good.[109] (7) Let them show the custom of loving purity; let them demonstrate the desire for meekness; let them make clear the gentleness of their tongue through silence.[110] Let them possess the same love for all who fear God without favoritism. (8) Let our children share in the instruction of Christ; let them learn how humility of mind prevails with God, what pure love can do with God, how important is revering him who is good and great, and how he saves all who turn completely to him with a pure mind.[111] (9) He is the searcher of thoughts and feelings whose breath[112] is in us, and whenever he wishes, he can take it away.

CHAPTER 22

(1) Faith in Christ confirms all these things. And he [Christ] calls us through the Holy Spirit in this way, "Come,

---

107 Polycarp of Smyrna expresses a similar thought in *PolyPhil* 4:3. Both Clement and Polycarp reflect the thought of Heb 4:13.

108 "deserters from his will." The Greek words are drawn from the military vocabulary of the times.

109 This verse offers short statements summarizing Christian living the way Paul does in Rom 12:9-17. Each of Clement's pieces of advice is related. Fearing God and revering Christ mean respecting official leaders of the church, past and present. Here is the idea of living in continuity with the traditions handed down through the church. The task of every generation is to pass on the faith by instructing the young and encouraging those under our influence to embrace the good.

110 It is not clear who the "them" of this verse is. It may be the women or the young mentioned in the previous verse or both.

111 Like Paul, Clement urges fathers to instruct their children in virtuous behavior. See Col 3:20-21.

112 "breath" here is probably a reference to the Holy Spirit, or it may be more general as a reference to God giving us life. In Heb 4:12, the word of God is called the discerner of the feelings and thoughts of the heart.

children, listen to me and I will teach you the fear of the Lord. (2) Who is the one who desires life and loves to see good days? (3) Stop your tongue (from speaking) evil and don't let your lips speak with guile. (4) Turn away from evil and do good. (5) Seek peace and pursue it. (6) The eyes of the Lord are on the righteous and his ears [attentive] to their prayers. The face of the Lord is against those who do evil to destroy the memory of them from the earth. (7) The just man cried out and the Lord heard him. He [the Lord] delivered him from all his afflictions."[113] (8) "Many are the scourges of the sinner but mercy will surround those who hope in the Lord."[114]

CHAPTER 23

(1) The all-merciful and kind Father has compassion on those who fear him, distributing his graces gently and mildly to those who come to him with a simple mind. (2) So, let us not be double-minded, nor let our soul dream up fantasies about his superabundant and glorious gifts. (3) Let this Scripture be far from us where it says, "Wretched are the double-minded, those who doubt in their soul, who say, 'These are the things we heard in our fathers' [time] and, look, we have grown old and none of these has happened.' (4) O foolish ones! Compare yourselves to a tree! Take a vine [as an example]! First, it sheds its leaves, then comes the shoot, then the leaf, then the flower, and after this the unripe grape, then a bunch of grapes is present."[115] See how in a short time the fruit of the tree reaches maturity. (5) Truly, his purpose will be completed quickly and suddenly as Scripture testifies, "He will come and not delay,"

---

113 Chapter 22 is almost entirely a quotation from Ps 34:11-19 (LXX 33:12-18). Clement uses the Psalm to encourage the Corinthians that the path to harmony and justice lies in doing good and trusting God for the outcome.

114 Verse 8 comes from Ps 32:10 (LXX 31:10).

115 It is impossible to find this text in the canonical Scriptures, but the same text is quoted in the ancient homily formerly called *Second Clement* (ch. 11). Most scholars suppose that the text occurred in some apocryphal Jewish writings now lost.

and again, "The Lord will come suddenly to his temple, the Holy One whom you await."[116]

CHAPTER 24

(1) Let us consider carefully, beloved, how the Master constantly shows us the future resurrection.[117] He made the Lord Jesus Christ its first fruits when he raised him from the dead.[118] (2) Beloved, let us examine the resurrection that happens at the right moment.[119] (3) Day and night display resurrection for us. Night sleeps; the day arises. Day disappears and night comes. (4) Let us take the fruits. How and in what way does sowing happen? (5) The sower went out and cast each of the seeds into the ground. These seeds, falling into the dry and barren ground, are dissolved. Then, from this dissolution, the majesty of the Master's providence makes them arise, and from one seed more grow and bear fruit.[120]

CHAPTER 25

(1) Let us look more carefully at the paradoxical sign given in the eastern regions, that is, in Arabia. (2) There exists a bird called a Phoenix. This is a unique bird and lives five hundred years, and when its time to die arrives, it makes for itself a tomb of incense, myrrh, and other spices. When its time is fulfilled, it enters and dies. (3) When its flesh has decayed, a worm is born that nourishes itself on the secretions of the dead animal and grows wings. Then once it is old, it carries away its tomb where the bones of the previous one are. Carry-

---

116 The first quotation in this verse derives from Hab 2:3 and the second from Mal 3:1.

117 Beginning now in chapter 24, Clement deals with the resurrection by giving examples drawn from the regularities of nature and stories from mythology (see chapter 25).

118 See 1 Cor 15:20: "Christ has been raised from the dead, the first fruits of those who have slept."

119 Ehrman translates the phrase *kata kairon* as "time after time" and Holmes as "regularly occurs." Jaubert chooses "at a fixed time" (*au temps fixé*). All these are possible.

120 Even though Clement does not recount the parable of the Sower here, it is hard to imagine that he did not think of the natural process of sowing as related to his point. See Mk 4:3ff; Mt 13:3ff; Lk 8:5ff.

ing these, it makes its way from the regions of Arabia to Egypt, to the city called Heliopolis. (4) There in the daylight, while all look on, it places them on the pedestal of the sun, and in this way it makes a start to go back. (5) So the priests study the historical records and discover that it had come after five hundred years.[121]

CHAPTER 26

(1) Do we think it is a great marvel if the Creator of everything would perform a resurrection of those who have served him in holiness in the confidence of good faith when he shows us the greatness of his promise through a bird?[122] (2) He says somewhere, "You will raise me up, and I will confess you."[123] Also he says, "I lay down and fell asleep; I awoke, because you were with me."[124] (3) Again Job says, "You will raise up my flesh that has endured all these things."[125]

CHAPTER 27

(1) With this hope, let our souls be bound to the One who is faithful in promises and righteous in judgments. (2) He who commanded us not to lie cannot himself lie. Nothing is impossible for God except to lie.[126] (3) Let faith in him be rekindled within us, and let us consider that all things are near him.[127]

---

121 Clement's use of the legend of the Phoenix is drawn from literary knowledge of several Greek sources. It is not necessary to assume that Clement thought the story of the Phoenix to be historically true, though we cannot exclude that possibility. He may well have simply used an example commonly believed in his culture to stress that the idea of resurrection was not absurd, even to pagans.

122 Now Clement draws out the implication of the myth of the Phoenix by arguing from the lesser to the greater (a minori ad majorem). If the ancients could believe in life after death as embodied in the story of the Phoenix, why is it strange to believe that the true God could raise someone from the dead?

123 This exact combination of words is not found in the OT but is close to Ps 28:7.

124 Ps 3:5.

125 This appears to be a paraphrase of Job 19:26. These quotations from the OT are to show that the resurrection was anticipated before Christ came into the world.

126 See Heb 6:18: "it is impossible for God to lie." Chapter 27 reinforces the idea that God will not fail to accomplish what he promises.

127 That is, that nothing is outside of his power and concern for his creatures.

(4) With a word of his majesty he established everything, and he can abolish them with a word.[128] (5) Who will say, "What have you done? Or who will oppose the power of his might?"[129] When he wills, as he wants, he will accomplish all things and none of the things decreed by him will pass away.[130] (6) All things are in his presence and nothing escapes his will. (7) So, "the heavens tell the glory of God, and the firmament declares the work of his hands, day sends forth the message to day, and night declares knowledge to night, and there are no words or speech where their voice is not heard."[131]

CHAPTER 28

(1) Since all things are seen and heard, let us fear him and flee the impure desires of base[132] deeds that we may be sheltered from the coming judgments by his mercy. (2) Where can any of us flee from his mighty hand? What sort of world receives someone who has deserted him? Scripture says somewhere, (3) "Where shall I flee and where shall I hide from your face? If I ascend into heaven, you are there; if I go out to the ends of the earth, your right hand is there. If I make my bed in the depths, your Spirit is there."[133] (4) So where may one go or where can he escape from the One who embraces all things?[134]

---

128 It takes God only *one* spoken word to bring things into existence and likewise to dismiss them from existence.

129 Wisdom of Solomon 12:12 and 11:21.

130 Cf. Mt 5:18: "not one iota or jot will pass away from the law until all is fulfilled."

131 Ps 19:1-2.

132 The word *phaulos* can mean "simple, slight, or insignificant" but also "bad, evil, or base," as it does in Rom 9:11, Jn 3:20, and 5:29. It is used in this moral sense by the Stoic philosopher Epictetus, who lived in Rome at the same time as Clement and whose thought has affinities with Clement's theology.

133 The Greek is a paraphrase of Ps 139:7-10.

134 The notion of God as the One who embraces all things has affinities with Stoic thinking but is also consistent with biblical ideas (see Wis 1:7). For God having all-embracing intelligence, see Marcus Aurelius *Meditations* bk. 8 ch. 54.

CHAPTER 29

(1) Let us then approach him in holiness of soul, lifting up to him holy and spotless hands, loving our gentle and compassionate Father, who has made us for himself as part of his election.[135] (2) Thus is it written, "When the Most High divided out the nations, when he scattered the children of Adam, he established boundaries for the nations according to the number of angels of God. His people Jacob became the Lord's portion, Israel an allotment of his inheritance."[136] (3) In another place it says, "Behold, the Lord takes a nation for himself from the midst of the nations, as a man takes the first fruits of his threshing floor. And from this nation the Holy of Holies will come."[137]

CHAPTER 30

(1) Since we are the portion of the Holy One,[138] let us do everything consistent with holiness, fleeing evil speech, vile and unholy entanglements, drunkenness, along with youthful and disgusting passions. Let us flee foul adultery and abominable arrogance. (2) For it says, "God resists the proud but

---

135 Holmes translates this last clause with a slightly different nuance, "who made us his chosen portion." My translation suggests that the purpose of God's election is union with him (for himself).

136 An exact quotation from the LXX version of Deut 32:8-9. The Hebrew text of Deuteronomy has "the number of the children of Israel" instead of "the number of angels of God." The idea that each nation has an angel assigned to it is found in later Jewish writings. Lightfoot argues that the LXX wording is probably the original in the early Hebrew text of Deuteronomy and that the OT is teaching that there is an angel assigned to each nation. The same idea lies behind the salutations of the seven letters of Revelation where the letter is addressed "to the angel of the church of …" (Rev 2:1,8,12,18; 3:1,4,7). This is one beginning of the idea of a guardian angel.

137 This quotation appears to be taken from some unknown work, but its wording is drawn from several canonical texts: Deut 4:34; Num 18:27; Jer 2:3; Ezek 48:12; Deut 14:2. The "Holy of Holies" could be a messianic reference, meaning that the Messiah will be like a new Holy of Holies, the original having been in the tabernacle in the desert and in the temple.

138 The MSS vary. Some say "holy portion," and so Holmes and Kleist translate it thus. The meaning is that, like Israel, the church of the new covenant is God's portion or inheritance.

gives grace to the humble."[139] (3) So let us join ourselves to those to whom the grace from God has been given. Let us clothe ourselves with harmony of mind, being humble and self-controlled, keeping ourselves far from all slander and evil speech, justifying our lives[140] by works and not by speech. (4) For he says, "He who says much will be heard in turn. Or does he who speaks eloquently think of himself as righteous? (5) Blessed is the one born of woman who has a short life. Don't be long with words."[141] (6) Let our praise be in God and not from ourselves for God hates those who praise themselves.[142] (7) Let the witness of our good lifestyle[143] be given by another, as it was given about our righteous fathers. (8) Rashness, stubbornness, and recklessness are [characteristic of] those who are cursed by God. Gentleness, humility, and meekness are [designed] for those blessed by God.

CHAPTER 31

(1) Let us join ourselves to his blessing and let us look at the ways in which he blesses. Let us unfold the events that have been from the beginning. (2) For what reason was our father, Abraham, blessed? Was it not because he practiced justice and truth through faith?[144] (3) With confidence, Isaac was willingly

---

139 Prov 3:34; Jas 4:6; 1 Pet 5:5.

140 "justifying our lives" could also be translated "being justified by…" (Holmes), or "let us seek justification…" (Kleist), or "let us be just…" (Jaubert). Clement's use of the verb *dikaioo* is difficult to discern. Does it mean "to be justified" in the theological sense that Paul uses it in the NT or simply "to act or live justly"? If the verb is intended as a passive form, then Clement is speaking about being justified by works. With this reading, Protestant commentators see Clement's doctrine of justification as inconsistent with Paul's. But is it inconsistent with the entire NT doctrine, including James's (see Jas 2:14-26)? Holmes (Protestant) and Kleist (Catholic) give different translations in accord with their differing doctrines of justification. Jaubert's "let us be just" may be closest to Clement's meaning, in that he is drawing out what it means to clothe oneself with humility, self-control, modesty in speech, and just actions rather than words.

141 A quotation from Job 11:2-3. Some translate "he who speaks eloquently" as "he who is talkative."

142 See also Rom 2:29; 1 Cor 4:5.

143 "lifestyle" translates *praxis*, which is normally rendered "deed" or "practice."

144 I agree with Jaubert in translating *poiesas* as "practice" rather than with Holmes'

led forth as a sacrifice because he knew the future.[145] (4) With humility, Jacob left his native land because of his brother and traveled to Laban to serve him. To him was given the scepter of the twelve tribes of Israel.[146]

CHAPTER 32

(1) If anyone sincerely considers God's gifts one by one, he will realize the magnificence of the gifts that are given by him. (2) From him[147] the priests and Levites and all the ministers stand at the altar of God. From him also the Lord Jesus comes in his humanity. From him also are kings, rulers, and leaders in the line of Judah. The remaining scepters[148] do not exist in small glory, as God promised, "Your seed will be like the stars in the sky."[149] (3) All have been glorified and magnified, not through themselves, or their works, or their righteous practices that they accomplished, but through his will. (4) So we too, called through his will in Christ Jesus, are not justified through ourselves, or our wisdom, understanding, piety, or even works performed in holiness of heart, but through faith. Through this, the Almighty God has justified them all from eternity. To him be glory forever. Amen.

CHAPTER 33

(1) What shall we do, brothers? Shall we simply refrain from doing good and neglect love? May the Master never al-

---

"attain."

145 Jaubert cites ancient texts which show that the Jews of the first century A.D. had already interpreted the sacrifice of Isaac as voluntary on his part, something not mentioned explicitly in Genesis 22 but which may be inferred. So, it is not surprising that Clement would pick up on this tradition. It means, of course, that not only was Abraham acting in faith, as is stated in Heb 11:17-19, but Isaac too was looking to the future with confidence.

146 Clement enumerates the three great patriarchs of Israel (Abraham, Isaac, Jacob) in keeping with the self-identification of God that he is the God of these three (e.g., Ex 3:6,15; 6:3,8). Here Clement emphasizes that in all three patriarchs, faith and action were united in obedience to God.

147 I.e., Jacob.

148 The scepters representing the other tribes of Israel.

149 Gen 15:5; 22:17.

low this to happen to us! Let us hasten to complete every good work with eagerness and zeal. (2) The Creator and Master of all rejoices over all his works. (3) By his all-majestic power he established the heavens, and with incomprehensible understanding[150] he put them in order. And he separated the land from the surrounding water and secured them on the sure foundation of his will.[151] By his order he commanded there to be animals roaming about on it. When he prepared the sea, he enclosed the creatures within it by his own power. (4) Above all, as the most excellent and greatest of all[152] he formed a man as a stamp of his own image with his holy and immaculate hands. (5) Thus God says, "Let us make man in our image and likeness. And God made man; male and female he made them. (6) When he completed all these things, he added his approval and blessed them by saying, "Increase and multiply."[153] (7) See! All the just were adorned in good works, and the Lord himself, once he adorned himself with good works, rejoiced. (8) Since we have this example, let us approach his will without hesitation, and let us perform the work of righteousness with all our strength.

CHAPTER 34

(1) The good worker receives the bread of his labor with confidence. The lazy and idle do not look their employer in the face. (2) We must be ready to do good, for all things come from him. (3) He told us before, "Behold, the Lord and his reward

---

150 The word *sunesis* is sometimes translated "wisdom" (Holmes), but I have chosen "understanding" to distinguish it from the normal Greek word for wisdom, *sophia*. Clement's statement that the creation came about from an incomprehensible understanding probably refers to God's knowledge, although it may also refer to the ultimate incomprehensibility of the creation itself. Moderns tend to assume that if we simply had enough time we could understand the entire universe. The ancients were more circumspect.

151 Clement affirms, as do the biblical authors, that the natural world runs according to God's plan for everything. Like Christians, the Greek and Roman Stoics believed in divine providence.

152 Some translators add "of his intelligence" because some ancient MSS contain this phrase.

153 Gen 1:22.

are before him to render to each according to his work."[154] (4) He urges us who believe not to be useless nor to be idle about doing good. (5) Let our boast and our confidence be in him. Let us submit to his will. Let us consider the entire company of the angels, that is, how they serve standing ready to do his will. (6) Scripture says, Tens of thousands stand before him and thousands upon thousands serve him and cry out, "Holy, holy, holy is the Lord of Sabaoth. The whole creation is full of his glory."[155] (7) We too gather in one place in harmony of conscience as we cry wholeheartedly to him with one voice that we may become partakers of his great and glorious promises. (8) For he says, "Eye has not seen nor ear heard nor has it entered into the human heart what he has prepared for those that wait for him."[156]

CHAPTER 35

(1) Beloved, how blessed and marvelous are the gifts of God! (2) There is life in immortality, splendor in justice, truth in boldness, faith in confident affirmation, self-control in holiness. All these things fall under our reasoning. (3) So, what are the things being prepared for those who endure? The Creator and Father of the ages, the all-holy One, knows their quantity and their beauty. (4) So, let us struggle to be found in the number of those who endure, that we may receive the promised gifts. (5) How can these things be, beloved? If our reason is established with respect to God through faith, if we seek out the things that are pleasing and acceptable to him, if we accomplish those things appropriate to his flawless will and follow the way of truth, then we can cast away from ourselves

---

154 Clement's words do not correspond to any specific biblical text but are close to Is 40:10 and Rom 2:6.

155 Is 6:3 has been an essential part of the church's liturgy from the earliest times because the liturgy is a union of heaven and earth.

156 Clement quotes 1 Cor 2:9 but changes the last phrase to "those that wait for him" from Paul's "those that love him." Paul in 1 Cor 2:9 says that he is quoting, but no one can find a precise quote in the OT to correspond to his words, though Is 64:4 has similar expressions.

all injustice and evil, greed, strife, as well as evil practice and malice, gossip and slander, hatred of God, arrogance and pretentiousness, empty glory and inhospitality.[157] (6) Those who practice such things are hateful to God, "not only they who do them but they who approve them."[158] (7) For Scripture says, "To the sinner God says, why do you speak of my righteous commandments and take up my covenant in your mouth, (8) but you hate correction[159] and throw my words behind you. If you see a thief, you run with him, and you throw in your lot with adulterers. Your mouth is filled with evil and your tongue weaves deceit. You sit satisfied while speaking against your brother, and place a stumbling block before your mother's son. (9) You did these things and I remained silent. O lawless man, you supposed that I would be like you.[160] (10) I will rebuke you and oppose you to your face. (11) Understand these things, you who forget God, lest you be snatched away and there is no one to rescue you. (12) A sacrifice of praise will glorify me, and there is the way by which I will show him the salvation of God."[161]

CHAPTER 36[162]

(1) This is the way, beloved, in which we found our salvation, Jesus Christ, the high priest of our offerings,[163] the protector and helper of our weakness.

---

157 Verse 35:5 is unclear in Greek. I have translated it with all the evil things mentioned being in the "then" clause (apodosis) of the sentence. Holmes leaves the issue unresolved, while Jaubert inserts the words "this will be so" before the first "if." In my solution, I am suggesting that putting away all the evil practices listed is based on faith and obedience to God's will.

158 A paraphrase of Rom 1:32.

159 The meaning of *paideia* hovers between "correction" and "instruction."

160 This sentence would make more sense as a question, but none of the MSS or printed editions punctuates it as such.

161 The second half of chapter 35 (vv. 7-12) is an extensive quotation from Ps 50:16-23.

162 Chapter 36 has the appearance of a christological hymn similar to Paul's in Phil 2:5-10.

163 Jesus Christ as "the high priest of our offerings" shows Clement's awareness of and dependence on the Letter to the Hebrews. See Heb 2:17ff and Heb 4:15.

(2) Through him we fix our gaze on the heights of heaven.
Through him we contemplate[164] as in a mirror his unblemished and incomparable countenance.
Through him the eyes of our heart have been opened.
Through him our unenlightened and darkened understanding shoots up toward the light.
Through him the Master willed for us to taste of immortal knowledge.

"He is the outshining of the Father's majesty, and, inasmuch as he is greater than the angels, he has inherited a much better title."[165] (3) Thus it is written, "He makes his angels spirits and his ministers a flame of fire."[166] (4) But of the Son, the Master spoke this way, "You are my Son; today I have begotten you. Ask from me and I will give you the nations as your inheritance and the ends of the earth as your possession."[167] (5) And again he says to him, "Sit at my right hand, until I make your enemies a footstool for your feet."[168] (6) Who are his enemies? It is those wicked people who oppose his will.

CHAPTER 37

(1) Brothers, let us live as soldiers with all zeal in [following] his faultless orders. (2) Let us consider those who fight for our leaders, how orderly, how obediently, how submissively they accomplish their orders.[169] (3) Not all are commanders, commanders of thousands, of hundreds, of fifty, etc. Each in

---

164 The same word Paul uses in 2 Cor 3:16.

165 Here Clement takes two phrases from Heb 1:3-4. Though there was later debate about whether the Letter to the Hebrews should be included in the NT canon — probably due to the lack of a specific author being mentioned — Clement provides us with evidence that in Rome the letter was considered canonical very early in the history of the church.

166 Heb 1:7 and Ps 104:4.

167 Heb 1:5 and Ps 2:7-8.

168 Heb 1:13 and Ps 110:1.

169 Clement now compares the church to military service in which Christians are called to serve as soldiers. Picking up on the NT use of military themes (see 1 Tim 1:18), Clement urges the Corinthians to see themselves as soldiers in spiritual battle.

his own order completes those things ordered by the king and his leaders.[170] (4) The great cannot exist without the small, nor the small without the great. There is a certain intermingling in every respect and benefit in these [orders].[171] (5) Let us take our body [as an example]. The head is nothing without the feet nor the feet without the head. The least important members of our body are necessary and useful for the whole body.[172] Rather, all work together and employ a united obedience so that the whole body can be healthy [saved].[173]

CHAPTER 38

(1) Let our whole body be saved in Christ Jesus.[174] Let each be subject to his neighbor as was given in the gift given him.[175] (2) Let the strong care for[176] the weak, and let the weak respect the strong. Let the rich make provision for the poor, and let the poor give thanks to God that he has given him one who can

---

170 As an army has various ranks and assigned tasks, so the church has orderly ranks that cannot be overthrown or ignored. Paul makes the same point in 1 Cor 12:28-30 with the use of numbers ("first … second … third").

171 Commentators note how the two sentences of verse 4 reflect both Greco-Roman and Jewish cultures. Paul uses the corresponding verb for the word "intermingling" here in 1 Cor 12:24 to describe the interdependence of the various orders within the body of the church.

172 Clement's language is clearly drawn from Paul in 1 Cor 12:18-25.

173 In this chapter, Clement teaches that unity in the church is a *structured* unity that must recognize different charisms and levels of authority. He follows Paul's teaching in Rom 12:6, "We have different gifts in accord with the grace given to us."

174 Clement sees the salvation or preservation of the whole mystical body (the church) as the responsibility of every member. The Greek *sozetho* may also mean "preserve" (Grant) or "maintain" (Kleist), whereas Jaubert paraphrases "Let us assure the salvation of the whole body." I have chosen with Holmes the more theological term "save."

175 The way to ensure the salvation of the whole church is to live within the charism given to each member, not attempting to step over the proper boundaries. In this one verse we have the interdependence of the mystical and structural aspects of the body of Christ. See Kleist's note (n. 113) for the intense research on the church as the mystical body in the first half of the twentieth century, culminating in the 1943 encyclical *Mystici Corporis Christi* of Pius XII.

176 I am reading *temeleo* "to care for" with Jaubert. Most MSS have this reading, but Holmes and Lightfoot read *me athmeleo* as "do not neglect." In the end, the meaning is the same.

fulfill his need.[177] Let the wise show his wisdom not in words but in good deeds. Let the one who is humble not testify about himself, but let others give testimony about him. Let the one who is pure in his flesh not boast, knowing that he who supplies his self-control is another.[178] (3) So brothers, let us carefully consider what material we came from, what sort of people and who we were when we came into the world, from what sort of tomb and darkness our Maker and Creator brought us into his universe. He prepared these acts of kindness[179] before we were born.[180] (4) Since we have all these things from him, then, we ought to give thanks to him in everything. To him be the glory forever and ever. Amen.

CHAPTER 39

(1) Those without wisdom and knowledge, those who are foolish and uninstructed, scoff and ridicule us, wanting to exalt themselves in their own minds. (2) What can a mere mortal do, and what power has an earthborn man?[181] (3) For it is written, "There is no form before my eyes, but I heard more of a breeze and a sound. (4) What then? A mortal cannot be pure before the Lord, can he? Or can a man be blameless from the works he does if he does not trust his servants, and considers

---

177 Clement's social ethic is thoroughly Pauline, using even the same language that Paul does. See Rom 12:4ff; Phil 2:30.

178 Clement warns against the demon of pride that lurks around the possession of positive virtues. Wisdom, humility, and continence (sexual purity) are laudatory but can lead to a feeling of superiority in the one who possesses them. Pride has long been considered one of the seven capital or deadly sins because it gives rise to so many other sins.

179 Most translators render *euergesia* as "benefits," but it is not clear whether Clement is referring to God's acts of kindness in creating us or to those acts which he enjoined on the Corinthians in the previous verses. If the latter, his meaning seems similar to Paul's in Eph 2:10, "We are his work, created in Christ Jesus for good works that God prepared ahead of time that we would walk in them."

180 By reminding the Corinthians of their lowly origins, Clement hopes to counter any temptation to pride because of receiving God's abundant gifts.

181 The two questions in this verse may be part of the mocking words from the schismatics in Corinth, or they may be Clement's rhetorical question to suggest that the problem in Corinth is so advanced that it requires more than human strength.

something crooked in his messengers?[182] (5) Even heaven is not pure in his sight, let alone those who dwell in clay houses; we ourselves are made of the same clay.[183] He smashed them like a moth, and they did not live even from morning until evening. Because they were beyond helping themselves, they perished. (6) He breathed on them and they died because they had no wisdom. (7) Call out and [see] if anyone listens to you[184] or if you see any of the holy angels. For anger will destroy the senseless man, and jealousy brings death to those deceived. (8) I have seen the foolish putting down roots, but their way of life is suddenly destroyed. (9) May their children be far from safety! Let them be mocked at the doors of the lesser, and there will be no one to rescue them. What is prepared for them, the righteous will eat. But they will not escape the evil [consequences]."[185]

CHAPTER 40

(1) Since these things are clear to us and we have peered into the depths of divine knowledge, we ought to do in an orderly fashion everything that the Master commanded us to fulfill in the properly established times.[186] (2) He commanded that the offerings and liturgical services[187] be fulfilled, not in

---

182 Quoted from Job 4:16-18 in the LXX.

183 Job 15:15.

184 Or it could mean "if anyone obeys you."

185 Job 4:19-5:5. Chapter 39, with its extensive quotations from the book of Job, forms a kind of lament found in the Bible and other ancient literature. It forms the background for Clement's attempt to address the problem of sedition and schism that begins in chapter 40.

186 Chapter 40 is significant for several reasons. It begins Clement's solution to the Corinthians' problem of schism. It also shows that at such an early date in the church's history, there were regular, set times for worship and prayer. It also shows that the worship of the early church was not open-ended and spontaneous. There was a definite structure of liturgy in Corinth to which Clement could appeal and which is in evidence in Paul's letter (1 Cor 11:23ff). This kind of structured worship is also seen in another of the earliest documents of Christianity, the *Didache*. See chapters 9, 10, and 14, where guidelines for the liturgy are specified (pp. 146-148 and p. 150 below).

187 The word *leitourgia* originally meant "public (civil) service" but was adopted by the early church to designate its worship because it was a public service for the

empty or disorderly ways, but at predetermined seasons and hours. (3) But where and by whom he wants it to be fulfilled he himself determined by his sovereign will, so that everything done in pleasing him may be acceptable to his will. (4) Those who make their offerings in the appointed seasons are acceptable and blessed, for they do not go astray when they follow the commandments of the Master. (5) To the high priest belong particular liturgical services; the priests have their own place, and the Levites have their own ministries too. The layman is given orders appropriate for the laity.[188]

CHAPTER 41

(1) Let each of you,[189] brothers, please God[190] in his own proper place with a good conscience by not transgressing the determined rule of ministry in dignity.[191] (2) It is not everywhere, brothers, that perpetual sacrifices are offered, or prayers or [those] for sin and faults. It is only in Jerusalem. Even there it is not in every place that they are offered but only before the temple at the altar. The offering is inspected for defects by the high priest and the ministers previously mentioned.[192] (3)

---

people of God. Paul used the word in the NT in 2 Cor 9:12; Phil 2:17,30.

188 Here we have the first known use of the word "laity" in the sense of distinguishing it from the clergy. Clement uses the OT offices of high priest, priest, and Levite, but clearly he is discussing the structure of the church in the new covenant. Early on, the clergy of the NT church is conceived of in sacerdotal terms.

189 Some MSS have "us" here.

190 I have followed the text in Jaubert (thus "please God") rather than Holmes ("give thanks to God"). Most of the MSS have Jaubert's reading.

191 Chapter 41 clearly shows that the church should always follow the proper order of government and worship because they have their origin in God's will. The word translated "proper place" is tagma or "order." In Clement, the clergy and laity are in properly distinct "orders" (tagma). This continues the emphasis of the NT on proper structure and order of the church. This applies to church leaders, as the Acts of the Apostles clearly testifies (see Acts 6:1; 13:1-3) or to worship, as Paul's directives in First Corinthians (ch. 11-14) show.

192 The reference to sacrifices in Jerusalem in 41:2 has been taken as evidence that this letter was written before A.D. 70, when the temple was destroyed. However, Clement may only be appealing to the OT teaching on Jerusalem as the proper place for worship to reinforce that the church should follow this example of worshiping as God has ordered it. Some scholars have suggested that temple worship continued in Jerusalem after A.D. 70 even though the temple was in a ruined state.

Those who do anything beyond his set will have a penalty of death. (4) See, brothers, the more worthy of knowledge we are, the more danger we come under.

CHAPTER 42

(1) The apostles received the gospel for us from our Lord Jesus Christ, and Jesus Christ was sent from God. (2) So Christ was from God, and the apostles from Christ. So both came by the will of God in good order.[193] (3) Once they received commands,[194] once they were made confident through the resurrection of our Lord Jesus Christ, and once they were entrusted with God's word,[195] they went out proclaiming with the confidence of the Holy Spirit that the kingdom of God would come. (4) Preaching in lands and cities, by spiritual discernment, they began establishing their first fruits, who were bishops and deacons[196] for future believers. (5) And this was nothing new because for many ages it had been written about bishops and deacons, as Scripture says somewhere, "I will appoint bishops for them in justice and deacons in faith."[197]

CHAPTER 43

(1) What amazement is it if those, who in Christ have been entrusted by God with such work, have appointed those who

---

Whatever the case, Clement is clearly viewing the worship of the church as a sacrificial act, a belief that is also reflected in the early Christianity of the *Didache* (see 14:1-3) and that will grow in the awareness of the church through time.

193 Clement teaches that the government of the church is of divine origin. The apostles' authority derives from God. He will develop this idea further in chapter 44, where he teaches apostolic succession. Here he wants to show that rebellion against legitimate authority is rebellion against God, an idea Paul teaches in Rom 13:1ff. The idea of the apostles being sent with authority by God is found also in Jn 17:18 and 20:21.

194 There are many words for "commands" in Greek. This one (*paraggelia*) carries the connotation of those given by a military superior to a subordinate.

195 Ehrman translates this phrase "persuaded by the word of God," and Jaubert translates it "strengthened by the word of God." Two reasons for choosing "entrusted with" are that it fits the chapter better, and *pistothentes* often carries the meaning of "entrust" as in 2 Tim 3:14.

196 Paul uses the phrase "bishops and deacons" in Phil 1:1.

197 Clement's quotation is a loose rewording of Is 60:17 as found in the LXX.

have been previously mentioned?[198] This was [in that place] where the blessed Moses, who was a faithful servant in all his house,[199] signified[200] all the commands given him in the sacred writings. The rest of the prophets followed him too by adding their own witness to the things legislated by him. (2) When jealousy about the priesthood arose within the tribes [of Israel] in rebellion, as to which of them would be adorned with the glorious name, that man [Moses] commanded the twelve leaders of the tribes to bring rods inscribed with the names of each tribe. Taking them, he wrapped them up and sealed them with the signet ring of the tribal leaders and put them in the tent of the testimony on the table of God. (3) When he shut the tent, he sealed both the keys and the rods. (4) He said, "Brothers, whichever tribe's rod buds, that is the one God has chosen to serve as priests and to minister to him. (5) The next morning he called together all Israel, six hundred thousand men. He showed the tribal leaders the seals and opened the tent of the testimony and brought forth the rods. The rod of Aaron was found not only to have budded but to have fruit on it.[201] (6) What do you think, beloved? Didn't Moses know ahead of time what would happen? Surely he did. But he did this that there might not be any disorder in Israel so that the name of the true and only [God] might be glorified. To him be glory for ever and ever. Amen.

---

198 Clement now proceeds to show from the OT that the appointed leaders of God's people should be honored, leaders of both ancient Israel and of the church.

199 A quotation from Heb 3:2, which in turn is quoting from Num 12:7.

200 "signified" or "made a sign of." Most translations soften the verb *esemeiosato* to "wrote" or "recorded." Quacquarelli retains the root meaning of the verb by the using the Italian verb *segnare*. In the context, Clement seems not to be saying that Moses wrote down the commands in the Scriptures, but that the case of the budding rod that he will cite is a confirmatory sign of the commands in Scripture.

201 See Num 17:1-13 (Mt 17:17-28) for the story of the budding of Aaron's rod. Clement's very loose recounting of the story is intended to show how God confirms the choice of his servants who rule over the people of God. It implicitly likens the rebellious Corinthians to the children of Israel who challenged the priesthood of the tribe of Levi. In both cases, the people of God are called to submission to rightful authority.

CHAPTER 44

(1) Our apostles knew from our Lord Jesus Christ that there would be contention over the title of the bishop's office. (2) For this reason, having received perfect foreknowledge, they appointed those mentioned before and afterwards gave the provision[202] that, if they should fall asleep, other approved men would succeed their ministry.[203] (3) Now as for those appointed by them [the apostles], or by other men of high reputation with the approval of the whole church, that is, those who have ministered without blame to the flock of Christ with humility, quiet, and beyond-perfunctory service,[204] those who are well attested by all for a long time, we do not consider it right to eject them from the ministry.[205] (4) It will be no small sin against us if we eject from the bishop's office those who have offered the gifts[206] without blame and with holiness. (5) Blessed are the presbyters who have gone before us who had a fruitful and perfect departure[207] for they no longer run the risk

202 This last phrase "gave the provision" is translated by Holmes as "afterwards gave the offices a permanent character." Jaubert notes that the meaning of *epimone* has been heavily disputed. The Vulgate gives "law" as its functional equivalent. See Jaubert, p. 172, n. 2.

203 Clement gives clear testimony to his belief in apostolic succession. The verb he uses here (*diadechomai*) and its related noun (*diadoche*) will be the standard terms in Christian Greek to designate this doctrine. For another early expression of apostolic succession, see Irenaeus *Against Heresies* bk. 3 ch. 3 sec. 3.

204 The Greek word translated "beyond-perfunctory service" is translated by Jaubert as "with dignity" and by Hemmer as "with distinction." Grant, Holmes, and Kleist translate it as "unselfishly." *Abanausos* derives from *banausos*, which means "mechanical." Clement seems to be saying that their service in the ministry is more than a matter of duty.

205 The word "ministry" translates *leitourgia*, the same word Clement uses for priestly service in the OT in 43:4.

206 The connection of offering the gifts with the bishop's office suggests that the pastoral ministry involved sacrificial ideas early on in the church. This connection would become more explicit later on as the notion of eucharistic sacrifice developed, but it was already present in the letters of Ignatius of Antioch. See a reference to the bishop's altar in Ignatius's *Letter to the Philadelphians* 4:1 and the discussion of the Eucharist in my *Ignatius of Antioch and Polycarp of Smyrna*, pp. 48ff.

207 "a fruitful and perfect departure" means that they faithfully fulfilled their priestly ministry.

of someone removing them from their established position. (6) For we see that you have removed some who have ruled well from a ministry that is honored by their blameless lives.[208]

CHAPTER 45

(1) Brothers, you are striving and zealous for those things that tend toward salvation.[209] (2) You have looked deeply into the holy Scriptures, the true writings [given] through the Holy Spirit. (3) You know that there are no wrong or false statements written in them. You will not find the righteous rejected by holy men. (4) The righteous were indeed persecuted, but it was by lawless men. They were imprisoned, but it was by the impious. They were stoned by lawbreakers. They were killed by those overcome with a foul and unrighteous jealousy. (5) In suffering these things they bore them famously. (6) What should we say, then, brothers? Was Daniel thrown into the den of lions by those who feared God?[210] (7) Or were Ananias, Azariah, and Mishael enclosed in the fiery furnace by those engaged in the majestic and glorious worship of the Most High?[211] No, certainly not! Who are those who have done such things? Hateful men, who are full of all evil and such great wrath that they tortured those who serve God with a holy and blameless resolve because they do not know that the Most High is the defender and protector of those who worship his all-virtuous name in a pure conscience. To him be glory forever and ever. Amen. (8) Those who endure in confidence have

---

208 Chapter 44 makes it clear that the order of offices in the church (bishop, priest, deacon) derive from divine authority. Some may discharge their duties well, and some may not, but the office is always to be honored.

209 The verb *este* can be translated "you are" (indicative) or "be" (imperative). The commentators are divided. Kleist and Quacquarelli translate it as indicative ("you are") while Lightfoot, Holmes, Jaubert, and Grant translate it as an imperative ("be"). In fact, Grant translates the verbs in verses 2 and 3 as imperatives also, "study" (v. 2) and "bear in mind" (v. 3). Although either is possible, I have chosen the indicative in my translation because it seems to fit the context a little better.

210 See Dan 6:16ff.

211 See Dan 3:19ff. The Hebrew names are Shadrach, Meshach, and Abednego.

inherited glory and honor. They were exalted and inscribed by God in his book of memory forever and ever. Amen.

CHAPTER 46

(1) Brothers, it is to such examples as these that we should unite ourselves. (2) For it is written, "unite yourselves to the holy ones because those who are joined to them will become holy."[212] (3) And again it says in another place, "With an innocent man you too will be innocent and with a chosen man, you too will be chosen, and with a twisted man, you will also become twisted."[213] (4) So let us unite ourselves to the innocent and the just. These are the elect of God. (5) Why then are there strife, fights, divisions, schisms, and war among you?[214] (6) Do we not have one God, one Christ, and one Spirit of grace poured out on us, and one calling in Christ?[215] (7) Why do we pull apart and tear Christ's members and foment rebellion in our own body[216] so that we end up in such insanity that we end up forgetting that we are members of one another? Remember the words of our Lord Jesus, (8) who said, "Woe to that man. It would have been better for him if he had not been born than to scandalize one of the elect. It would be better for him to have a millstone hung about him and to be plunged into the sea than to turn one of my elect away."[217] (9) Your schism has turned many away. It has thrown many into discouragement,[218] many into disorder, and all of us into sorrow. Your rebellion is persisting.

---

212 The source of this quotation is unknown. Clement quotes it as if it were from Sacred Scripture but no one has been able to find this saying anywhere in Scripture. Here is a possible early expression of the idea that friendship with the saints who have gone before are an active help in our earthly pilgrimage.

213 Ps 18:25b-26 (LXX 17:26b-27).

214 See Jas 4:1.

215 Clement adopts Paul's teaching on unity in Eph 4:1-3.

216 I.e., the body of the church.

217 Clement combines Mt 26:24 and Lk 17:1-2.

218 *Athumia* may be stronger than "discouragement." It may be "despair."

CHAPTER 47

(1) Take up the epistle of the blessed Paul the apostle. (2) What did he first write in the beginning of the gospel?[219] (3) In truth, he sent you a letter in the manner of the Spirit[220] about himself, Cephas, and Apollos, because at that time you created dissensions.[221] (4) But that dissension brought you a lesser sin, for you took the part of the attested apostles and of a man approved among them.[222] (5) But now think about those who have distorted you and lessen the dignity of your famous brotherly love. (6) It is shameful, indeed, very shameful, and things unworthy of your conduct in Christ to hear of the very solid and ancient church of the Corinthians because one or two persons are fomenting rebellion against the presbyters.[223] (7) And this report has reached not only us, but others who differ from us, so that blasphemies against the Lord's name are piled on because of your folly. And it is producing danger for you.

CHAPTER 48

(1) So, let us remove this quickly and fall before the Master and weep, entreating him that by being merciful to us, he would reconcile us and restore us to a holy and pure prac-

---

219 Meaning the first proclamation of the gospel to the Corinthians.

220 I follow Jaubert's interpretation of *pneumatikos* "under the inspiration of the Spirit."

221 *Prosklisis* usually means "proclivities" or "leanings." Holmes and Grant choose "factions," Kleist "factious agitation," while Hemmer and Jaubert translate it "plots" (*cabale*). Quacquarelli chooses "formed parties." In the context, it clearly means something more than proclivities.

222 Clement is referring to 1 Cor 1:10-18 and 3:4 where Paul counters the factionalism among members of the Corinthian church who claimed, "I belong to Paul" and "I belong to Apollos" and "I belong to Cephas." Paul, like all other NT writers, sees schism within the church as contrary to the will of God. The purpose of the church is to break down the dividing walls that people put up against one another (see Eph 2:14-16).

223 "presbyters" is the word *presbuteros*, which meant "old man" or "elder." It was adopted in the NT as a designation for an office in the church and is translated "elder" in many Protestant versions. Catholic and Orthodox translations typically transcribe rather than translate the word, as I have here. In this view, "presbyters" was an early word for "priests."

tice of brotherly love. (2) This is the gate of righteousness that stands open to life, as it is written, "Open to me the gates of righteousness. Entering in them, I will confess[224] the Lord. (3) This is the gate of the Lord; the righteous will enter in it."[225] (4) Of the many open gates, this is the one of righteousness that is in Christ. In this [gate], those who enter and who make their way in holiness and righteousness are blessed, completing everything without disturbance. (5) Let a man be faithful; let him be able to explain knowledge; let him be wise in discerning words; let him be pure in deeds. (6) He ought to be the more humble the greater he seems to be, and he ought to seek the common good and not what is good for himself.[226]

CHAPTER 49

(1) Let the one who has love in Christ practice the commands of Christ.[227] (2) Who can draw out the bond of the love of God? (3) Who is sufficient to tell the greatness of his beauty? (4) The height to which love leads is indescribable. (5) Love joins us to God, love covers a multitude of sin,[228] love bears all things, endures all things. There is nothing base in love, nothing arrogant. Love does not contain division; love does not foment rebellion.[229] Love does all things in harmony. In love, all the elect of God are made perfect. Without love, nothing is pleasing to God.[230] (6) It is in love that the Master has taken

224 Kleist and Jaubert choose "praise."

225 These quotations come from Ps 118:19-20.

226 See Phil 2:5.

227 Chapters 49 and 50 are Clement's praise of Christian love in imitation of Paul's treatment of love in 1 Cor 13. Clement paraphrases some of Paul's language but adds other phrases that focus on the sin of schism and division.

228 "Love covers a multitude of sin" is a quote from 1 Pet 4:8 or Jas 5:20. Both NT texts are quotations from Prov 10:12, though neither the NT authors nor Clement gives it as the Greek of the LXX has it. In Clement's use, the phrase means that love does not account wrongs and sins against it. Love is the opposite of hate.

229 Division (schism) and rebellion are contrary to the nature of God's love because obedience and love are always united as in Jn 14:15,21.

230 This summarizes Paul's teaching in 1 Cor 13:1-3; even heroic deeds or superior knowledge mean nothing without love.

us[231] to himself. It was because of the love that he had for us that Jesus Christ, our Lord in the will of God, gave his blood in our behalf. He also gave his flesh for our flesh[232] and his soul for our souls.[233]

CHAPTER 50

(1) Beloved, see how great and wonderful love is; the perfection of love is beyond all telling. (2) Who is worthy to be found in it except the one whom God makes worthy?[234] So, let us ask and beg this from his mercy that we may be found in love without human division,[235] i.e., blameless.[236] (3) All generations from Adam to this day have come and gone, but those who have been perfected in love possess a place with the godly by the grace of God.[237] These are the ones who will be manifested in the visitation of the kingdom of Christ. (4) For it is written, "Enter into the caves bit by bit until my wrath and anger pass by. And I will remember a good day and raise

---

231 The verb could be translated as "drawn us to himself" as Jaubert takes it (French *attirer*).

232 Clement may be thinking of the death of Christ on the cross or perhaps the Eucharist, but in either case Christ gives his blood and body to the Church.

233 The mention of Christ giving his soul plays into the later controversies about whether Christ possessed a rational human soul. Origen of Alexandria thought that the Eternal Logos took the place of the human soul in Christ. Apollinaris of Laodicea denied that Christ had a fully human rational soul. This teaching was formally condemned by the second ecumenical council of Constantinople in 381.

234 This chapter emphasizes that the kind of love needed in the church is not of human origin or power. It is God's grace poured into the church that makes love possible.

235 Clement's word for "division" is *prosklisis*, which can also be translated "partiality" (Grant). Other translators choose stronger terms (e.g., "factiousness" — Holmes, and "*cabal*" — Jaubert). *Prosklisis* generally means "a tendency to create something," in this context, division. See also n. 221.

236 Here "blameless" explains further what Clement means by "without human division." Love in the church works toward unity, not division. But full unity is not possible through human strength alone. It requires the divine love that is poured out in response to the church's cry for mercy.

237 In chapter 49, Clement spoke of God's elect as being perfected in love. Now he reaffirms this truth. Clearly, his view of love implies that it is a virtue that grows through time, not a static position or ephemeral feeling. This draws on Paul's teaching that love is the greatest of the three theological virtues (see 1 Cor 13:13).

you up from your tombs."[238] (5) We are blessed, beloved, if we do God's commands in the harmony of love,[239] that our sins may be forgiven through love.[240] (6) It is written, "Blessed are those whose iniquities are forgiven and whose sins are covered. Blessed is the man to whom the Lord does not impute sin nor is guile found in his mouth."[241] (7) This blessing came upon those chosen by God through Jesus Christ our Lord. To him be glory forever and ever. Amen.

CHAPTER 51

(1) In whatever ways we have fallen away and whatever we have committed because of the insinuations of the Adversary, let us be found worthy of forgiveness.[242] But those who are leaders of the revolt and schism ought to look into what is common to our hope.[243] (2) For those who conduct their lives with reverence and love would prefer to fall into insults rather than [have] their neighbors [do so] and would rather bear contempt for themselves than for that harmony which has been handed on to us so justly and well.[244] (3) For it is better for a man to make an open admission of his transgressions than to harden his heart, as the heart of those inciting rebellion against Moses, God's servant, was hardened. Their

---

238 This is not an exact quotation, but Clement seems to be combining Is 26:20 and Ezek 37:12.

239 Performing God's commands without love achieves nothing, as Paul stresses in 1 Cor 13:1-3. The "harmony of love" means the harmony that flows out of love and leads to love.

240 The mention of sins being forgiven through love is evocative of 1 Pet 4:8 and Jas 5:20. A similar thought can be found in Prov 10:12.

241 Quoted from Ps 32:1-2 and also quoted by Paul in Rom 4:7-8.

242 Chapter 51 follows the panegyric on love with a plea to confess the sin of schism and dissension. Repentance means seeking the common good of the church.

243 Kleist translates this "the common nature of our hope"; Jaubert *ce qui nous est commun dans l'esperance.*"

244 Verse 51:2 is not a clear sentence in the Greek original, but the last phrase about harmony being delivered to the church seems to refer to the command of the apostles to be united in the church, as Paul urged the Corinthians in 1 Cor 1:1-18. It also implies that the harmony and the unity of the church is not a creation of the church itself but a gift from above handed down through the apostles.

judgment is obvious. (4) "For while living they went down to Hades and death will rule[245] them." (5) Pharaoh, his army, and all the leaders of Egypt, their chariots and riders, all sank and perished in the Red Sea for no other reason than their uncomprehending hearts were hardened after the signs and wonders in Egypt through Moses, the servant of God.

CHAPTER 52

(1) Brothers, the Master of all lives without need of anything. He needs nothing from anyone except that they would confess him. (2) David, the chosen one, said, "I will confess the Lord, and it will please him more than a young bull bearing horns and hoofs. Let the poor see and be glad."[246] (3) And again he says, "Sacrifice to God a sacrifice of praise and offer to the Most High your prayers. Call on me in the day of your affliction, and I will deliver you, and you will glorify me."[247] (4) "The sacrifice [that pleases] God is a crushed spirit."[248]

CHAPTER 53

(1) You know, beloved, and you know very well the Holy Scriptures. You have peered into the words of God. We write these things to bring them to remembrance. (2) When Moses went on the mountain, staying there forty days and forty nights in fasting and humbling himself, God said to him, "Go down quickly from here because your people have acted lawlessly, those whom you brought out of Egypt. They quickly abandoned the way that I commanded them; they made for themselves molten images." (3) And the Lord said to him, "I have told you once and again twice. I have seen this people and, look, they are stiff necked. Permit me to destroy them and I will wipe away their name from under heaven. And you I will make you as a great and awesome nation much more numer-

---

245 A quotation from Ps 48:15 in the LXX. "Rule" is *poimanei*, which usually means "to shepherd" but is used in certain biblical texts in a negative sense.

246 Quoted from Ps 69:30-31.

247 Ps 50:14-15.

248 Ps 51:17.

ous than them."[249] (4) But Moses said, "No Lord! Forgive the sin of this people. As for me, wipe me out from the book of the living."[250] (5) O what great love! O what perfection beyond compare! A servant is bold with his Lord. He asks forgiveness for the multitude or asks that he himself be blotted out with them.[251]

CHAPTER 54

(1) Who among you is noble, compassionate, filled with love? (2) Let him say, "if because of me there is dissension, strife, and schism, I will leave, I will go where you want, and I will do those things commanded by the congregation. Only let the flock of Christ live in peace with the appointed presbyters.[252] (3) He who does this will gain a great honor for himself and every place will receive him, "for the earth is the Lord's and its fullness."[253] (4) Those who live this way have and will conduct themselves as God's citizens without regret.

CHAPTER 55

(1) To take some examples of the Gentiles, many kings and leaders, having received an oracle during a moment of pestilence, delivered themselves over to death that they might rescue their own citizens with their own blood. Many left their own cities that there might not be more rebellion. (2) We ourselves know many among us who have delivered themselves over to imprisonment that they may redeem others. Many have delivered themselves into slavery and, upon receiving their money, have fed others. (3) Many women, being empowered by God's grace, acted valiantly by doing many manly

---

249 Deut 9:13-14.

250 Ex 32:32.

251 Clement invokes the example of Moses as a model for the servants of God. Those in rebellion against the presbyters should emulate his sacrificial love for the church's welfare.

252 Lightfoot cites texts which show that the idea of voluntary exile here in Clement was quoted by the Syriac fathers later. Jaubert adds that the same theme is to be found among the Stoics. See Jaubert, p. 33.

253 Ps 24:1.

things. (4) Blessed Judith, during the siege of her city, asked from the elders permission to go out into the camp of [their] enemies. (5) Exposing herself to danger, she went out because of her love for her country and for the people being besieged. The Lord delivered Holofernes into her feminine hands.[254] (6) Esther, perfect in faith, exposed herself to no less danger that she might rescue the twelve tribes of Israel about to be destroyed. Through her fasting and humility, she considered the all-seeing Master, the Eternal God, worthy.[255] God, seeing the humility of her soul, rescued his people, for whose sake she exposed herself to danger.[256]

CHAPTER 56

(1) So let us intercede for all those who are in a transgression, that docility and humility may be given, so they yield, not to us, but to the will of God. In this way, their remembrance of God and the saints will be fruitful and perfect combined with mercy.[257] (2) Beloved, let us take correction at which no one ought to feel irritated. The admonishment we give to one another is pleasing and especially profitable because it unites us to the will of God. (3) A holy saying expresses it thus, "With correction, the Lord corrected me and did not deliver me over to death."[258] (4) "He whom the Lord loves, he corrects. He chastises every son whom He receives."[259] (5) "The righteous will correct me in mercy and will rebuke me. Let him

---

254 See Judith chapters 8-13 and her hymn of praise in 16:5-9. Clement's use of this story suggests that for him, the book of Judith was possibly canonical.

255 Most translate *exiose* by some strong verb of asking such as "entreat" or "implore." I have chosen to remain closer to the root sense of "deem or count worthy." Esther showed her faith by counting the God of Israel worthy of her deepest entreaties.

256 Clement's summary is recapping the entire book of Esther.

257 This simple sentence admits of different meanings. I have translated it such that the prayers of those being prayed for would not be hindered by their rebellion. The mention of mercy in remembering "the holy ones" suggest prayers for the faithful departed, i.e., saints not in the ultimate sense of those who have attained to the blessed vision of God but for those who are on the journey to God.

258 Ps 118:18.

259 Prov 3:12.

not anoint my head with the oil of sinners."[260] (6) Again it says, "Blessed is the man whom the Lord admonishes. Do not reject the admonishment of the Almighty for he himself inflicts pain but again restores. (7) He struck but his hands healed. (8) Six times he will rescue you from necessary [distress], but the seventh time evil will not touch you. (9) In famine he will rescue you from death, and in war he will deliver you by his iron hand. (10) He will hide you from the whipping of the tongue, and you need not fear the evil that will come. (11) You will laugh at the unrighteous and the lawless; you need not fear wild beasts. (12) Wild beasts will make peace with you. (13) Then you will know that your house will be at peace. Your way of life in your dwelling will not err. (14) You will know that your posterity will be abundant and your children will be like the grass of the field. (15) You will enter the tomb like ripe wheat being harvested at the proper time or like a pile at the threshing floor being collected at the proper hour."[261] (16) Look, beloved, how great is the protection for those being disciplined by the Master. As a good father, he disciplines that we may receive mercy through his holy discipline.

CHAPTER 57

(1) So you, having laid the foundation of this rebellion,[262] submit to the presbyters and allow yourselves to be instructed for repentance as you bow down the knees of your heart. (2) Learn to submit by casting off arrogance and the proud stubbornness of your tongue. It is better for you to be found small and accountable among the flock of Christ than to appear excellent and be cast away from his hope. (3) An all-virtuous wisdom speaks like this: "Behold, I will pour forth a deliverance of my breath and I will teach you my word. (4) Since I

---

260 Ps 141:5 (LXX 140:5). Clement, as always, quotes from the LXX, which differs somewhat from the MT as we have it now.

261 Job 5:17-26.

262 Lightfoot has "Ye therefore that laid the foundation of the sedition, submit yourselves unto the presbyters and receive chastisement unto repentance, bending the knees of your heart."

called and you did not obey and since I extended my words and you did not heed but rather rendered my counsels of no authority, you disregarded my rebukes. Therefore, I too will laugh at your destruction, and I will rejoice whenever destruction comes to you and when confusion comes suddenly to you. This catastrophe will be like a present storm, or whenever affliction and anguish come on you. (5) And it will happen that whenever you call on me, I will not hear you. Evil men will seek me and they will not find me, for they hated wisdom and they did not choose the fear of the Lord. Nor did they want to heed my counsels, and they sneered at my counsels. (6) Therefore, they eat the fruits of their way and are filled with their own impiety. (7) Because they treat babies unjustly, they will be slaughtered and a visitation will destroy the ungodly. But the one who hears me will dwell in hope with confidence and he will live in quiet without fear from every evil."[263]

CHAPTER 58

(1) Let us obey his all-holy and glorious name by fleeing the aforementioned threats to the disobedient [made] through wisdom that we may dwell confidently on the most holy name of his majesty. (2) Receive our counsel and you will regret nothing. For God lives and our Lord Jesus Christ lives and the Holy Spirit [lives],[264] the faith and hope of the elect, because the one who has practiced the requirements and commands given by God in humility with an intense virtue will be in good order and enrolled among the number of the saved through Jesus Christ, through whom is glory to him [the Father] forever and ever. Amen.

---

263 Prov 1:23-33.

264 During Clement's time, in the 90s of the first century, the doctrine of the Trinity had not yet been consciously formulated by the church, but his mention of the three Persons of the Trinity shows that the Nicene formulation in A.D. 325 drew on Scripture and the earliest tradition of the church.

CHAPTER 59

(1) If some are disobedient to the things said by him through us, let them know that they will involve themselves in not a little transgression and danger.

(2) As for us, we will be innocent of this sin and will with intense request and entreaty ask for the Creator of all to preserve the number of his elect throughout the world unharmed through his beloved child, Jesus Christ our Lord.[265] It was through him that he called us from darkness to light, from ignorance to the knowledge of his glorious name.

(3) Give us, Lord, to hope in your original name of all
    creation,[266]
You have opened the eyes of our hearts to know you,
You who alone are the Most Exalted in the heights,
Resting holy among the holy ones.[267]
[You are]
The One who humbles the pride of the arrogant,
The One who destroys the reasoning of the nations,
Who lifts up the humble into the heights and humbles the
    exalted,

---

265 Verse 59:2 now introduces a long prayer that many scholars see as drawing on the Roman liturgy. One indicator is Clement's use of *pais* ("beloved servant" or "child"), which is used as a designation of Jesus in other early Christian prayers (see Acts 3:13,26; 4:27; *Didache* 9:2-3; 10:2). The liturgical flavor of this prayer is reinforced by the closing doxology in 61:3. This, together with the liturgical flavor of chapters 9, 10, and 14 of the *Didache*, suggests that there was a fairly set liturgy early in the ancient church though there were undoubtedly local variations.

266 The construction of this clause (i.e., "to hope," etc.) is unusual in Greek and suggests that Clement may have lifted this directly from the liturgy. To speak of the "original name of all creation" may mean that God placed his stamp on the created order by imparting his presence to it. The physical world reflects the Creator's trustworthiness, which is what chapter 20 emphasizes. See Ps 19:1-7. "Give us, Lord" is an insertion suggested by Lightfoot to make sense of this sentence.

267 "the holy ones" may refer to either humans perfected in holiness (i.e., saints) or to angelic beings. In either case, the picture is one of God as the king among the heavenly court. Here is another indicator of the liturgical origins of this prayer. The phrase "remaining holy among the holy ones" occurs in the *Liturgy of St. Mark* used in Alexandria and in the *Liturgy of St. John Chrysostom* in Constantinople. See the Greek text in C.E. Hammond, *Antient Liturgies* (Piscataway, NJ: Gorgias Press, 2004), pp. 94, 178.

Who enriches and impoverishes,
Who gives death and makes alive.[268]
[You are]
The only Benefactor of spirits,[269] and the God of all flesh,
Who sees into the abyss,
Observer of human works,[270]
The Helper of those in danger,
The Savior of those in despair,
The Creator and Overseer[271] of every spirit,
You who fill the nations upon the earth,
You who choose from among all those who love you through
    Jesus Christ,
Your beloved child.
Through him you have taught,[272] sanctified, and honored us.[273]

(4) We deem you worthy, O Master, to be our Helper and our
    Protector.
Save[274] those of us in distress,[275]
Raise the fallen,

---

268 These last five lines reinforce the biblical theme of God turning the tables on
    human pride, a theme prominent in Hannah's song in 1 Sam 2:1-10 and Mary's
    Magnificat in Lk 1:46-55. Similarly, 1 Pet 5:5-6 and Jas 4:6-7 emphasize that God
    gives grace to the humble while resisting the proud.

269 It is not clear whether "spirits" here refers to the spirits of human beings or to
    preternatural spirits, whether good or evil. In either case, adding "God of all flesh"
    suggests that Clement sees God as the Sovereign Master.

270 In the sense of weighing human actions for merit or demerit.

271 The word "overseer" here is the same word used for "bishop" in the NT and early
    Christian writings, i.e., *episkopos*. God is the original overseer whom every bishop
    should emulate.

272 Grant chooses "disciplined" rather than "taught" here. The word *paideuo* means
    a systematic teaching over time, e.g., a course of study. Our word "pedagogy"
    derives from it.

273 God has shown honor to the human family in addressing our intellects by teach-
    ing and our souls by sanctifying grace.

274 Now in 59:4 Clement uses the imperative forms to plead with God for what the
    church needs. These pleas are based on God's providential mercy, which was cel-
    ebrated in the titles ascribed to him in verse 3. All liturgies in the church alternate
    between the recognition of who God is and prayer for the needs of the church.

275 Some MSS add, "Be merciful to the lowly."

Show yourself to the needy,
Heal the sick,
Turn back those among your people who are deceived.
Feed the hungry,
Rescue our prisoners,
Raise up the weak,
Comfort the fainthearted.[276]
Let all the nations know you[277]
That you alone are God,
And that Jesus Christ is your child
And "we the people of your pasture."[278]

CHAPTER 60

(1) For you have made clear the everlasting structure of the
  cosmos through the things made.[279]
You, O Lord, created the inhabited world;
you are faithful in all generations,
righteous in judgments,
wonderful in strength and majesty,
wise in creation and sagacious,[280]
establishing what has come to be,
good in the visible realities

---

276 From "raise the fallen" to "comfort the fainthearted," these pleas for mercy reflect
the biblical picture of God who attends to the needs of the deprived and weak.
See, e.g., Ps 146:7-9. Since God is attentive to the needy, the church should also
be. So important is the care of the poor that Jesus makes it a basis for the final
judgment in Mt 25:31-46.

277 "Let all the nations know you" reflects the church's desire for the universal (catho-
licity) of the faith and the gospel. The church's universality was inherited from the
Hebrew Scriptures, where the people of the covenant desired the true God to be
known and worshiped by every nation on earth. See Pss 67; 96; 98.

278 Ps 79:13; Ps 100:3.

279 Chapter 60 contains four types of prayer: (1) praise for the power and wisdom of
God in creation, (2) exultation of God's attributes (e.g., mercy, compassion, justice), (3) a plea for forgiveness in the light of these attributes, (4) a plea for peace
and harmony. All these elements show up in the historic liturgies of the ancient
church.

280 The creation reflects both God's power and wisdom. These last two lines are
similar to Ps 104:24.

kind[281] toward those who trust in you,
merciful and compassionate,
forgiving our iniquities,
injustices, transgressions, and faults.[282]

(2) Do not count all the sin of your servants and handmaidens
but cleanse us with the purity of your truth;
make straight our steps to walk in holiness of heart
and to do the things that are good and pleasing in your sight
and in the sight of our rulers.

(3) Yes, Master, shine your face on us for good things in peace,
that we may be protected by your mighty hand
and be rescued from our sin by your uplifted arm
and rescue us from those who hate us unjustly.

(4) Give harmony and peace to us and to all who live on earth
as you gave to our fathers when they called on you complete-
    ly in faith and truth,
becoming obedient to your all-powerful and all-virtuous
    name,
and to those who reign and guide us on earth.

CHAPTER 61

(1) You, O Master, have given the authority of the kingdom to
    them[283]
through your majestic and indescribable power
so that we would know the glory and honor given them by
    you[284]

---

281 Some MSS have "faithful" (*pistos*), which Holmes follows.

282 Some translate *plemmeleia* as "sins," but I have chosen "faults" in order to distin-
     guish it from *hamartia*, which is the normal Christian word for "sin."

283 Chapter 61 contains petitions for the pastors of the church that can be seen in all
     the historic liturgies (anaphora) of the church, both East and West. For example,
     in the Roman Canon that developed after Clement's time we hear, "We offer them
     [the bread and wine] for your holy Catholic Church. Grant it peace, protect, help
     and rule it throughout the world together with your servant N, our Pope, and N,
     our bishop, and for all orthodox teachers of the catholic and apostolic faith."

284 Honor is due to bishops and other clergy because the authority given them
     derives from God's goodness, not the merits of the officeholders.

and that we would submit to them and do nothing to oppose your will.

Give to them, O Lord, health, peace, harmony, stability

that they may attend, without offence, to the leadership given by you.

(2) For you, O Heavenly Master, King of the Ages,

have given to the sons of men glory, honor, and authority over the things of earth.

You, O Lord, guide their decisions by what is good and pleasing in your sight

that, exercising the authority given them by you with godliness in peace and in meekness,

they may obtain your propitious mercy.

(3) [You are] the only One who can do these good things and more with us.

We confess you by the high priest and protector of our souls,[285]

Jesus Christ, through whom glory and majesty are yours now and forever and ever.

CHAPTER 62

(1) We have instructed you well enough, brothers, about those things fitting for our religion[286] and most useful for a virtuous life for those who wish to pursue a holy and just life. (2) We have handled every topic having to do with faith, conversion,[287] authentic love, self-control, discretion,[288] and perseverance, recalling that you should be completely pleasing to the Almighty God in righteousness, truth, and long-suffering. You should be united in love and peace, forgetting

---

285 See also 36:1 and 64:1.

286 "religion" is the broader meaning of *threskeia,* which in a narrower sense means "worship."

287 *Metanoia* is usually translated "repentance" in the NT and means literally a "change of mind or heart."

288 Holmes translates *sophrosune* as "sobriety," but the word has a broader application than the English word typically implies. It is a virtue that parallels self-control and self-possession.

evil [done against you] with earnest forbearance,[289] just as our forefathers, shown earlier, humbly did the things pleasing to the Father, the Creator God, and to all men. (3) We have reminded you of these things with much pleasure since we surely knew how to write to faithful, eminent men, well instructed in God's educative revelation.[290]

CHAPTER 63

(1) It is fitting with so many examples of this kind that we move toward bowing our necks and fulfilling our place of obedience that we may attain the goal lying before us in truth, without any defilement, by refraining from vain rebellion. (2) You will supply us with joy and gladness if, being by obedient to the things written by us through the Holy Spirit,[291] you root out the unlawful anger of your jealousy in accord with the entreaty that we made for peace and unity in this letter. (3) We sent men who have been living among us faithful and wise lives from their youth to old age, even blamelessly, who will act as witnesses between you and us. (4) We did this for you to know that [our] whole thought has been and is to bring peace among you quickly.

CHAPTER 64

(1) Finally, may the all-seeing God and Master of spirits and Lord of all flesh, who chose the Lord Jesus Christ and us through him to be a special people,[292] may he give to every soul

---

289 "with earnest forbearance" translates *meta ektenous epieikeias*, an unusual combination. It seems to mean that searching for harmony and unity requires persistent and gentle patience.

290 Chapter 62 summarizes the entire thrust of the letter's appeal to unity, harmony, and submission to legitimate authority. More than anything, Clement proposes a life of virtue as the way to these goals.

291 Verse 2 suggests that the Roman church had legitimate authority to command because it was guided by the Holy Spirit. See chapter 4 in the introductory essays.

292 "a special people" translates the biblical phrase *laon periousion*, which is used in Tit 2:14. A similar expression (*laos eis peripoiesin*) occurs in 1 Pet 2:9. Both these can be translated from the Hebrew word *segulah* or the phrase *am segulah* used in Ex 19:5, Deut 7:6, and 14:2, among others. *Am segulah* parallels "holy people" in these OT texts and means that Israel was chosen by God to be his special people

that is called by his majestic and holy name faith, reverence, peace, endurance and longsuffering, self-control, purity, and discretion so as to please his name through our high priest and protector, Jesus Christ. Through Christ is glory and majesty, power and honor to him [Father] now and forever and ever.

CHAPTER 65

(1) Send back to us quickly in peace and joy those sent from us, Claudius Ephebus and Valerius Biton, with Fortunatus, so that they may tell us more quickly of the peace and harmony that we so desire and pray for. (2) The grace of our Lord Jesus Christ be with you and with all who are called by God through him everywhere. Through Christ may glory, honor, power, and majesty, the eternal throne be to him forever and ever. Amen.[293]

---

or treasure. In applying these phrases to the church, Clement, like Peter in 1 Pet 2:9, means that the church of the new covenant is now the chosen people of God.

293 Clement here ends his letter with a benediction much like Paul does in his letters. See 2 Cor 13:13.

CHAPTER NINE

The Teaching[1] of the Lord for the Nations through the Twelve Apostles

The Ways of Life and Death Section

CHAPTER 1

(1) There are two ways, one of life and one of death, and there is a great difference between the two ways.[2] (2) This is the way of life.[3] First, you shall love God who made you; second, love your neighbor as yourself.[4] Everything that you

---

1   "Teaching" is *Didache*. Milavec translates this as "Training."

2   The Didachist contrasts two ways that were common in the Bible and in ancient Jewish literature. Psalm 1 stands at the beginning of the Psalter as a contrast between "the path of the wicked" and "the path of the righteous." This Psalm is a guiding theme for reading and praying the entire Psalter. Early Christians who nourished themselves on the Psalter imbibed the thinking of the OT and Judaism.

3   Now begins the explication of the way of life that lasts through chapter 4. This chapter shows that the way of life leading to Christian perfection goes beyond justice and requires mercy as the heavenly Father displays.

4   Deut 6:5. The Christian way of life leading to perfection goes beyond a justice which only gives just rewards. It means imitation of God the Father, who in his

wish not to be done to you, don't do to another.[5] (3) The teaching of these words is this: bless those who curse you and pray for your enemies.[6] Fast for those who persecute you. What merit[7] is it [for you] if you only love those who love you? Don't the pagans[8] do the same thing? But you should love those who hate you and you will have no enemies. (4) Abstain from fleshly and bodily desires. If someone gives you a slap on the right cheek, turn the other to him, and you will be perfect.[9] If someone presses you into service for one mile, go with him for two.[10] If someone takes away your garment, give him your tunic as well.[11] If someone takes from you what is yours, don't demand it back. For you are not even able to do so.[12] (5) Give to everyone who asks of you and don't demand [anything] back. For the Father wishes to give out of his own gifts to all [people].[13] Blessed is the one who gives in accord with the commandment for he is blameless.[14] Woe to the one

---

goodness does not discriminate between people. See Mt 5:43-48 and Lev 19:18.

5   This negative form of the golden rule corresponds to the positive form in Mt 7:12 (cf. Lk 6:31). Tobit 4:15 reads: "That which you hate, do to no one."

6   Cf. Rom 12:14: "Bless those who persecute you; bless and do not curse."

7   *charis* could also be translated "grace."

8   "pagans" here represents the Greek *ethne*. Normally translated "the nations," as in the title, or as "Gentiles," this word is used in the Bible to refer to those outside the commonwealth of Israel. Christians then used the term to refer to their non-Christian neighbors.

9   Mt 5:39 does not contain the addition, "you will be perfect," but one can easily see how it is implied. Polycarp's *Letter to the Philippians* (12:3) emphasizes that perfection consists of loving those who hate. See my translation and commentary in *Ignatius of Antioch and Polycarp of Smyrna*, p. 157.

10   Mt 5:41.

11   Mt 5:40.

12   Not being "able to do so" probably means that it cannot be done without violating the perfect law of love.

13   The word "gift" here is *charisma*, which is used by Paul with an awareness of its cognate charis ("grace"). Thus, Paul says that "the *charisma* of God is eternal life" (Rom 6:23) and that God gives to the members of the church various spiritual *charisma*ta (gifts) for the building up of the body (1 Cor 12:4).

14   "blameless" or "innocent." The word *athoos* only occurs twice in the NT (Mt 27:4,24), but *amomos* ("blameless," "without stain") is a synonym used eight times. See e.g., Eph 1:4.

who takes. If anyone who has a need takes something, he will be without guilt.[15] But the one who does not have a need will stand trial for what he took and why he did it. When he is in prison,[16] he will be interrogated about the things he has done. He will not be free until he pays back the last cent. (6) But this is what will be said about this [rule], "Let your alms sweat in your hands until you know to whom to give it."[17]

CHAPTER 2

(1) The second commandment of the teaching [is this].[18] (2) Do not commit murder,[19] do not commit adultery, do not corrupt youth, do not commit fornication, do not steal, do not practice magic, do not give drugs,[20] do not commit an abortion,

---

15 Here seems to be contradiction but only on the surface: a command not to steal followed by an exception to the rule. However, this was later formulated as the moral principle called the universal destination of all goods. Since in the eschaton no one will own any property (universal destination), in this life the one who has a genuine need has a right to claim material goods. The difficulty lies in judging when a need is genuine.

16 "prison" translates *sunoche*. I follow Rordorf's translation here.

17 The origin of this saying has never been found. Some scholars (e.g., Rordorf) see this limitation on generosity as contradicting the statement in v. 5 (cf. Mt 5:42) about unrestricted giving. Milavec argues that it is not a contradiction but a clarification and appeals to Augustine's comment on Ps 146:17, "You have heard one injunction just now: 'Give to everyone who asks you' (Lk 6:30); and in another place scripture says, 'Let your alms sweat in your hand until you find a deserving person to whom you can deliver it.' If one petitioner is seeking you out, you must go and seek another. This does not mean leaving the first one destitute … but you must still go searching for another." St. Augustine, *Expositions of the Psalms*, trans. Maria Boulding, vol. 6 (New York: New City Press, 2004), p. 437. The thought here in the *Didache* and in Augustine seems to be that the Christian should be generous and open-handed in giving to the needy but also be discerning about those who may wish to wrongly take advantage of such generosity.

18 Jewish, Christian, and Hellenistic writings all contained catalogues of vices to be avoided. Rom 1:29-30 contains such a list. See also *ClCor* 35:5 for Clement's list of vices.

19 Most of these prohibitions are found in the Decalogue in Ex 20 and Deut 5. Others are taken from other OT texts or are practices found in the pagan culture of the early church.

20 *pharmakeuo* is translated by Holmes as "engage in sorcery." The word is used for drugs in the practice of sorcery or more generally to administer harmful drugs to someone.

nor kill anything that has been born.[21] Do not desire your neighbor's property. (3) Do not swear a false oath,[22] do not bear false witness, do not use abusive language,[23] do not hold grudges against past wrongs.[24] (4) Do not be vacillating between two opinions or double-tongued, for being double-tongued is the snare of death.[25] (5) Let not your message be false, or empty, but rather full of deeds. (6) You shall not be a greedy person, or a thief, or a hypocrite, or malicious, or arrogant. Do not take part in an evil plan against your neighbor. (7) You shall not hate anyone. Rather, some you have to rebuke, others you have to pray for, and still others you should love above your own soul.

CHAPTER 3

(1) My child, flee from every evil and from everything that appears to be like it. (2) Do not be prone to anger for anger leads to murder. Don't be a jealous, quarreling, or violent person. From all these are born murders. (3) My child, don't be a lustful person for lust leads to sexual impurity. Don't use foul language or have wandering eyes[26] for from all these things adulteries are born. (4) My child, do not engage in soothsaying for it leads to idolatry. Be neither an enchanter, nor an astrologer, nor a defiler. Do not even desire to see such things. For from all these things idolatry is born. (5) My child, do not become a liar, for lying leads to stealing. Don't be a lover of mon-

---

21 From the earliest times, abortion and infanticide have been forbidden for the followers of Christ.

22 Or possibly "commit perjury" in a court of law. The prohibition here could be based on Mt 5:33ff.

23 "abusive language" translates *kakologeo*, the same word used in Mt 15:4, "he who verbally abuses his father and mother will die."

24 Discouraging the retention of grudges can be found in *ClCor* 2:5; 62:2, where harmony in love includes being without grudges that nurse anger.

25 Jas 1:8 is similar, "he is a double souled man, unstable in all his ways."

26 Holmes translates *aischrologos* as "foulmouthed" and *hupselophthalmos* "letting your eyes run." Rordorf translates the first as "obscene comments" and the second as "indiscreet glances." The second term (*hupselophthalmos*) occurs only here in Greek literature, and so its meaning is uncertain.

ey or vainglorious for from all these things come thefts. (6) My child, don't be a complainer because it leads to blasphemy. Don't be self-willed or fixed on bad things for blasphemies are born of these things. (7) But be meek for the meek will inherit the earth. (8) Be patient and merciful, guileless, quiet, good, always respecting the words which you have heard. (9) Do not exalt yourself or allow your soul to be impulsive[27] for your soul should not be joined to high things.[28] Rather conduct your life with just and humble [thoughts]. (10) You should accept the events that happen to you as good, knowing that nothing happens without God.

CHAPTER 4

(1) My child, night and day remember the one who speaks the word of God to you. Honor him as the Lord. For where the Lordship is spoken of,[29] the Lord is there. (2) You should seek out the faces of the holy ones[30] every day that you may rest upon[31] their words. (3) Do not produce a schism; make peace with those who are at odds. Judge with justice. Do not show favoritism to rebuke transgressions. (4) You should not be double-minded whether this should be or not. (5) Do not be one who stretches his hands out to receive and hesitates to give. (6) If you possess anything through working with your own hands, you should give it as a ransom for your sins.[32] (7)

---

27 Or perhaps "audacious." Holmes chose "arrogant" for *thrasos*, but the word seems to signify more impulsivity than pride. Ehrman's "impertinent" seems better.

28 Or possibly "people in high places." Focusing one's attention on high position or people produces vanity and pride.

29 Holmes has "where the Lordship is preached." Rordorf has "where his sovereignty is announced." In 2 Pet 2:10, Peter uses the same word *kuriotes* (lordship) when speaking of the condemned who "despise dominions."

30 "the holy ones" naturally raises the question whether the author meant angels, or holy men on earth, or the saints in heaven.

31 Ehrman has "find comfort in" rather than "rest upon," but in later patristic literature the word *epanapauo* means "to rest on, to rely on." See the entry in *A Greek Patristic Lexicon*, ed. G.W.H. Lampe (Oxford: Oxford University Press, 1961).

32 Both Jewish and Christian sources contain this idea: 1 Pet 4:8 ("love covers a multitude of sins") paraphrases Prov 10:12. Polycarp has a similar exhortation: "When you are able to do good, do not put it off because alms liberate from death,"

Do not hesitate to give; nor grumble when you do give for you know who the good paymaster of the reward is. (8) Do not turn away from the needy; you should share all things with your brother and call nothing your own. If you are sharers in what is immortal, how much more [should you be] in mortal things![33] (9) Do not withhold[34] your hand from your son or daughter but from their youth teach them the fear of God.[35] (10) You should not give commands to your male or female servants in your anger — they hope in the same God — lest they completely stop fearing the God of you both. For he [Christ] does not come to call by high reputation,[36] but he prepared those whom the Spirit has prepared. (11) And you servants, be subject to your masters in shame and fear[37] as if they were God's representative.[38] (12) You should hate all hypocrisy and everything that does not please the Lord. (13) Under no circumstances neglect the Lord's commands. Guard what you have received, neither adding nor subtracting anything.[39] (14)

PolyPhil 10:2.

33   A truth emphasized in Acts 2:43-47; 4:32-35.

34   Rordorf, Holmes, and Ehrman see it as "withholding discipline." The verse seems to enjoin the delicate combination of positive instruction and necessary discipline.

35   Verses 9 to 12 have to do with the domestic responsibilities of Christians; they align with Paul's instructions in Col 3:22-4:1 and Eph 6:4-9.

36   *kataprosopon* means with regard to a person's social status. God's call in Christ cuts across all social strata.

37   I.e., ashamed to disobey and respect for the master's position.

38   *Hos tupo theou* could also be rendered "as the stamp of God." Holmes has "a symbol of God" and Ehrman "a replica of God." Their more literal renderings still mean that the master is God's representative, much like Paul speaks of government in Rom 13:1-5.

39   The prohibition against adding or subtracting from God's commands is also found in Deut 4:2 and Rev 22:18.

In the church[40] [liturgy] confess your transgressions,[41] and you should not come to prayer with an evil conscience. This is the way of life.[42]

CHAPTER 5

(1) This is the way of death. First of all, it is evil and fully cursed: murders, adulteries, lusts, acts of sexual immorality, stealing, idolatry, magical arts, sorceries,[43] robberies, false prophecies, hypocrisies, double-mindedness, guile, arrogance, evil,[44] insolence,[45] greed, filthy speech, envy,[46] audacity, self-exaltation, bragging.[47] (2) [This way has] persecutors of those who are good, hating truth, loving a lie, ignoring the reward of righteousness, not uniting [themselves] to good and righteous judgment, looking out not for good but for what is evil. Meekness and patience are far from people like these who love futile things, while pursuing a reward; they have no mercy on the poor, put out no effort for the oppressed, and do not know him who made them. They are murderers of children, corruptors of things made by God, turning away from the needy, oppressing the afflicted, currying the favor of the rich, unjust judges of the impoverished, completely given over to sin. Children, be delivered from all these things.

---

40 The word *ekklesia* occurs four times in the *Didache*. See chapter 7 above in the introductory essays for further discussion. Here it seems to signify "assembly," the root meaning of the word in Greek. Thus, I have added the word "liturgy" because it seems implied. Rordorf cites texts that show that the Qumran community publicly confessed their sins in their assemblies. The liturgies of the Eastern churches later had public confession as well. This practice is, of course, still present in the historic churches of the East and the West (e.g., the *Confiteor*).

41 Confessing one's sins in the assembly of the faithful occurs again in 14:1.

42 Here ends the first major section in contrasting the ways promised in 1:1. Verse 1:2 began explicating "the way of life." Now, the author in chapter 5 explicates the "way of death."

43 *pharmakiai* could also be the administration of drugs in general. See note 20.

44 *kakia* is translated as "malice" by Ehrman and Holmes.

45 That is, audacity to the point of pugnacity.

46 *zelotupia* generally means jealousy, rivalry, envy.

47 The word *alazoneia* is used in 1 Jn 2:16 in the phrase "the boastful pride of everyday life." It signifies an arrogant attitude about one's possessions and position.

CHAPTER 6

(1) Watch out lest someone cause you to stray from this way of teaching since he teaches you apart from God.[48] (2) If you can bear the whole yoke of the Lord, you will be perfect.[49] If you cannot, do whatever you can. (3) Concerning the matter of food, bear whatever you can. Especially abstain from meat offered to idols for it is worship of dead gods.[50]

The Liturgical Section

CHAPTER 7

(1) Concerning baptism, baptize in this way.[51] When you have said all these things,[52] baptize into the name of the Father, of the Son, and of the Holy Spirit[53] in running water.[54] (2) If you don't have running water, baptize in another water. If you cannot do so in cold [water], do so in warm. (3) If you

---

48 Chapter 6 is a transition from the teaching on the two ways to the liturgical portion of the *Didache*, in chapters 7-10. He summarizes the way of life as taking on the yoke of the Lord. The Didachist has clearly understood that taking the yoke of Christ means living according to his commands and thereby internalizing his meek and gentle heart.

49 A clear allusion to Mt 11:29-30, where Jesus says, "Take my yoke upon you and learn from me for I am meek and humble of heart ... for my yoke is gentle and my burden light." The text in Mt 11 says nothing about being perfect, but in Mt 5:44-48 Jesus teaches that perfection is to love like the heavenly Father, i.e., even to the unappreciative and unrighteous.

50 The Didachist's language seems similar to that in 1 Cor 8:1-13 where Paul calls all pagans gods no gods at all. Eating in a pagan temple could cause a weaker Christian to fall even though eating meat offered to an idol is not really wrong because the idols are nothing.

51 Here begins the liturgical section of the *Didache*, which extends through chapter 10. It deals with the two most important sacraments (baptism, Eucharist) as well as devotional practices that surround the liturgy (fasting, prayer).

52 "all these things" appears to mean preparatory prayers for baptism, much like the Preface of the Canon was later used in eucharistic prayers. It may also refer to the teaching of the two ways that is in chapters 1-6. Here we have evidence of a pre-baptismal catechesis at a very early stage of the church's history.

53 Cf. Mt 28:19. Assuming the *Didache* is the earliest Christian document outside the NT, this is the first explicit reference to trinitarian baptism in church history.

54 The phrase "running water" may also mean "living water" (*hydor zon*) as it is usually translated in Jn 4. In the second instance of this verse "running water" is clearly more appropriate, but the author is probably intentionally picking up on this double meaning to emphasize that baptism conveys life. See Rom 6:1ff.

have neither, pour out [water] on their head into the name of the Father, of the Son, and of the Holy Spirit.[55] (4) Before the baptism, let both the baptizer and the one baptized fast and others too as they are able. You shall command the one being baptized to fast for one or two days.

CHAPTER 8

(1) Do not practice fasting with the hypocrites.[56] They fast on Mondays and Thursdays. You should fast on Wednesdays and Fridays.[57] (2) Nor should you pray like the hypocrites. Rather pray as the Lord commanded in his Gospel:[58]

Our Father, who are in heaven.

Hallowed be your name.

Your kingdom come.

Your will be done on earth as it is in heaven.

Give us today our daily bread.[59]

---

55 This may be the first instance of an alternative to immersion in the mode of baptism. Through time, immersion or christening (on the head) would become acceptable modes. The most essential thing is use of water and the trinitarian formula.

56 This is probably a reference to Jewish fasting days. In the probable context of a Jewish Christianity, the Didachist urges distinguishing Christian practice from Jewish.

57 Rordorf points out that later on the Egyptian monks held catecheses on Wednesdays and Fridays, when fasting was supposed to take place.

58 The form of the Lord's Prayer here is almost exactly the same as in Mt 6:9-13, with two exceptions noted below.

59 There is a long history of interpreting "daily bread" as referring to the Eucharist. The Greek word *epiousios* is an enigma. Early on, some church fathers read it as consisting of *epi* ("above") and *ousios* ("substantial" or "of an essence") and was translated into Latin as *supersubstantialis*, meaning that this bread was of a heavenly origin and above all created substances. Thus it was taken to refer to the bread of life as Jesus speaks of it in John chapter 6. Jerome says in his *Commentary on Matthew* bk. 1 ch. 6: "'Give us today our supersubstantial bread' ... But we have expressed out loud supersubstantial, in Greek *epiouson* which word the Septuagint interpreters very frequently translate as *periousion* (special). Thus, we have looked at the Hebrew and wherever they choose *periousion*, we have discovered the Hebrew word *segola*, which Symmachus translated *exaireton* (precious, chosen), that is, special or particular, distinguished or extraordinary although in certain texts it is interpreted as peculiar (unique). So when we ask for God to give us that peculiar or special bread, we are asking him who said, 'I am the living bread who came down from heaven' [Jn 6:51]."

Forgive us our debt[60] as we forgive[61] our debtors.
Lead us not into temptation but deliver us from evil.
For yours is the power and glory forever.
Pray this three times a day.[62]

CHAPTER 9

(1) Concerning the Eucharist, celebrate the Eucharist in this way.[63] (2) First, concerning the cup, we thank you, our Father, for the holy vine of David your servant which you made known[64] to us through Jesus your child.[65] To you be the glory forever. (3) Concerning the broken bread, pray like this: "We thank you, our Father, for life and knowledge that you have made known to us through Jesus your child. To you be the glory forever. (4) As the broken bread was scattered on the mountains and then gathered into one, thus let your church be gathered from the ends of the earth into your kingdom[66] because yours is the glory and the power through Jesus Christ

---

60 Mt 6:12 has "debts" (*opheilemata*), while the Didachist uses "debt" (*opheile*).

61 Mt 6:12 uses the perfect "have forgiven" (*aphekamen*), while the Didachist uses the present "forgive" (*aphiemen*).

62 The admonition to pray at least three times a day is an early indication of what would later become the Liturgy of the Hours, i.e., times of the day set aside for prayer. We know from Acts 3:1 and other sources that the Jews had fixed hours of prayer prior to Christians.

63 The terms "Eucharist," "celebrate the Eucharist," and "we thank" are all from the root verb *eucharisteo* and can be translated simply "thanksgiving," which is its meaning taken by scholars who do not see any liturgical background here. But the noun *eucharistia* here seems already to be a technical term for the liturgy, unlike the use of the same word in the NT. I side with those scholars (e.g., Rordorf) who see this as an early form of the eucharistic liturgy. See the discussion in chapter 7 of the introductory essays.

64 That is, "revealed." The Eucharist celebrates the coming of Jesus Christ as the final revelation of God in Christ. See Heb 1:1-3.

65 The word *pais* can be translated as either "servant," as I have done in the case of David, or as "child" as in the case of Jesus. It is used to refer to both as God's child/servant in the prayers of Acts. See Acts 3:13; 4:25-27.

66 Every celebration of the Eucharist includes a plea for the unity of the church, a theme that endures to this day. This connection is evident in 1 Cor 10:17, "Since there is one bread, we many are one body for we all partake of the one bread." Ignatius of Antioch (ca. A.D. 107) speaks in similar terms of the connection between unity and the Eucharist in his *Letter to the Ephesians* 20:2. See my discussion above in chapter 7 of the introductory essays.

forever." (5) Let no one eat or drink from your Eucharist except those who are baptized in the name of the Lord.[67] For the Lord said about this, "Do not give holy things to dogs."[68]

CHAPTER 10

(1) After this is fulfilled, give thanks[69] like this. (2) We thank you, Holy Father, for your holy name, which you have made to dwell in our hearts,[70] and for the knowledge, faith, and immortality which you made known to us through Jesus your child.[71] To you be glory forever. (3) You, Lord Almighty, have created all things for your name's sake. You have given food and drink to men for enjoyment that they may thank you. But you have graciously given us spiritual food and drink and eternal life through your child.[72] (4) Above all, we thank you that you are mighty. To you be glory forever. (5) Remember, Lord, your church, to rescue it from every evil and to make it perfect in your love,[73] and from the four winds gather it completely sanctified into your kingdom which you have prepared for yours is the power and glory forever.[74] (6) Let grace come

---

67 This restriction on who may receive the Eucharist became the standard in later centuries because the sacrament signifies union with the church. Those not baptized are not yet in union with the church. The sacred meal is designed for Jesus's disciples only, as he himself gave it to them in the upper room (see Mt 26:20-29).

68 Cf. Mt 7:6. As in Matthew's Gospel, this saying was apparently a proverb in Jewish culture that must not be taken too literally. The Didachist sees the meaning of the proverb as guarding the sanctity of the Eucharist from distribution to those not prepared to receive it (i.e., the non-baptized). This is a sacred obligation.

69 Here I have translated the same verb as in 9:1 (*eucharistesate*) differently because here it seems to retain its original meaning of "give thanks." The corresponding noun in 9:5 clearly must bear the meaning of a technical term, i.e., Eucharist.

70 The name of the trinitarian God is placed in the heart of the believer through baptism.

71 See note 65.

72 In the divine arrangement (economy of salvation), spiritual life is conveyed in a manner similar to natural life, i.e., through eating and drinking.

73 The prayer for the deliverance of the church from evil and the perfection of its holiness is found in most of the ancient liturgies. It endures even to today. Being "perfect in love" means that the liturgy of the church is designed for the complete sanctification of the faithful. See also 16:2.

74 The pilgrim church on earth always has its eyes set on the eternal kingdom to be revealed in the return (*parousia*) of Christ. As in 9:4, the celebration of the Eucha-

and this world pass away. Hosanna to the God of David.[75] If anyone is holy, let him come.[76] If anyone is not, let him repent. Maranatha! Amen. (7) Permit the prophets to give thanks whenever they wish.[77]

The Church Order Section

CHAPTER 11

(1) Whenever someone comes and teaches all the things mentioned before, receive him. (2) If the teacher himself turns away and teaches another doctrine so as to destroy [what should be taught], do not listen to him. But [if it] adds to righteousness and knowledge of the Lord, receive him as the Lord. (3) Now concerning apostles and prophets, do what is in accord with the doctrine (dogma) of the gospel. (4) Let every apostle who comes to you be received as the Lord. (5) He [should not] stay but one day. And if there is [a special] need, one more day. If he stays three days, he is a false prophet. (6) Let the apostle who leaves, take nothing but bread until he finds lodgings. If he asks for money, he is a false prophet. (7) Do not test and evaluate every prophet speaking in the Spirit. For every sin will be forgiven, but this sin will not be forgiven.[78] (8) Not everyone speaking in the Spirit is a prophet but [only] if he has the ways of the Lord.[79] It is from the ways [of living] that the false prophet and the [true] prophet are

---

rist contains prayer for the unity of the church.

75 Mt 21:9 and 15 have "Hosanna to the Son of David." *Hosanna* is a Greek transliteration of the Hebrew *hoshiana* ("save now") of Ps 118:25. It is a plea for help and salvation. The Jewish people who welcomed Jesus entering Jerusalem with these words were making a plea for salvation from the Son of David. The *Didache* shows how early this plea, which endures to this day, was incorporated into the liturgy of the church.

76 Not holy in and of himself but made so through repentance and forgiveness.

77 Of course, *eucharistein* here could mean "to hold Eucharist."

78 See also Mt 12:31. Verse 7 is enigmatic. It seems that it should have no negative in it.

79 Meaning, as Ehrman translates more loosely, "who conducts himself like the Lord."

known. (9) Every prophet who limits the table[80] in the Spirit does not eat from it.[81] If he does, he is a false prophet. (10) Every prophet who teaches the truth, if he does not practice what he preaches, is a false prophet.[82] (11) Every true prophet, who has been approved, in performing the mystery of the church in this world[83] but not teaching to do what he does, will not be judged by you. His judgment lies with God, for the ancient prophets did likewise. (12) Whoever says in the Spirit, "give me money" or something else, do not listen to him. If he says [this] about others who lack something to give, let no one judge him.

CHAPTER 12

(1) Let everyone who comes in the name of the Lord be received. Then, once you test him, you will know and have understanding on the right and on the left.[84] (2) If the one coming is a traveler,[85] help him as much as you are able. He will not stay with you but two or three days if necessary. (3) If he wishes to stay with you, and is a craftsman, let him work and eat. (4) If he does not have a skill, make a provision in accord with your conscience, that is, how a Christian will live with

---

80   All existing translations render the phrase *horizon trapezan* ("limits the table") as something like "order a meal" or "ordering a dining table to be set" (Milavec). The expression is rare in Christian Greek, as Rordorf admits, and its meaning is not clear. See next note.

81   The situation envisioned here is not clear, but it may refer to a prophet who orders that a table should be set for the poor or that he forbids certain poor people from partaking of such a set table. In either case, he shows his true colors if he partakes of it himself. He is self-interested rather than concerned about the poor.

82   Mt 23:3: "Do and keep everything they [scribes] tell you to do but do not do as they do for they do not do what they teach."

83   "Performing the mystery of the church in this world" has been translated quite differently by various scholars. See my discussion of the phrase in chapter 7 of the introductory essays, on pp. 69-71.

84   I have chosen the more literal translation to retain its connection to biblical language such as Jn 4:11. Holmes and Ehrman use "what is true and what is false."

85   Milavec's and Rordorf's translation. Holmes and Ehrman have "simply passing through."

you without being idle. (5) If he does not want to do this, he is one who uses Christ for his own gain.[86] Beware of such people.

CHAPTER 13

(1) Every true prophet who wishes to stay with you is worthy of his food. (2) Likewise, a true teacher is worthy of his food like a worker. (3) Of all the first fruits of the products of the wine vat and the threshing floor, of cattle and sheep, give the first fruits to the prophets for they are your high priests. (4) If you do not have a prophet, give to the poor. (5) If you grow grain, take the first fruits and give according to the commandment. (6) Likewise, once you open a bottle of wine or oil, take the first fruit and give it to the prophets.[87] (7) In accord with the command, give the first fruit of money, clothing, and every possession, as seems right to you.

CHAPTER 14

(1) On the Lord's Day,[88] once you have gathered, break the bread [of the Lord], and celebrate the Eucharist,[89] after having confessed your transgressions[90] that your sacrifice may be pure. (2) Let no one who has a quarrel with his friend join you until they reconcile, that your sacrifice not be defiled.[91] (3) This is what was said by the Lord, "In every place and time offer to me a pure sacrifice because I am a great king, says the Lord, and my name is marvelous among the Gentiles."[92]

---

86 I.e., one who wishes to trade on the name of Christ for his own profit. *Christemporos* occurs only once in Greek literature, but its meaning is clear from its constituent parts (*Christos* = Christ, *emporos* = salesman).

87 These commands for giving first fruits are roughly like those in Ex 22:29-30.

88 This chapter seems somewhat out of place as it naturally goes more with chapters 9 and 10. Yet, it may be here to emphasize the activities appropriate for the Lord's Day. Rev 1:10 has a similar expression.

89 Holmes and Ehrman render *eucharistesate* as "give thanks," although the latter also offers "celebrate the Eucharist" as an alternative. See also n. 63.

90 See also 4:14 about confessing one's sins in the church liturgy.

91 The requirement for reconciliation with others is drawn from Mt 5:23-24.

92 A quotation from Mal 1:11. The Didachist version does not match exactly the biblical text. See the fuller discussion of this verse in chapter 7 (pp. 75-77 above).

CHAPTER 15

(1) Elect[93] for yourselves bishops and deacons worthy of the Lord, men [who are] meek, free from the love of money, true and tested. They will minister to you the ministry of prophets and teachers. (2) Do not despise[94] them for they are those who have been honored with the prophets and teachers. (3) Correct one another, not in wrath but in peace as you have it in the gospel. As for everyone who does wrong to another, let him not hear from you until he repents.[95] (4) Practice your prayers and almsgiving and all your deeds in this way, as you have it in the gospel of the Lord.[96]

The Section on the Final Things

CHAPTER 16

(1) Be vigilant about your life. Do not let your lamps be snubbed out nor your loins relaxed. Rather be prepared for you do not know the hour in which the Lord is coming. (2) You should gather frequently and seek those things appropriate for your souls. For the whole time [allotted] for your faith[97] will not profit you unless you are perfected in the final moment.[98] (3) For in the last days false prophets and corrupters

---

93 Holmes and Milavec give "appoint." Ehrman, Quacquarelli, and Rordorf choose "elect." Rordorf claims without explanation that the verb *cheirotoneo* does not carry the technical meaning of "ordain." Presumably this means that ordination involved more than the choice of candidates. Perhaps the Didachist envisions a situation similar to Acts 6:1-6, where the people nominated seven men for the apostles to lay their hands on, i.e., ordain.

94 All translators see a similar meaning in *huperidete*, except Ehrman, who softens it to "disregard."

95 This seems to be an application of Jesus's teaching on fraternal correction in Mt 18:15-17. A similar admonition is found in Ignatius of Antioch: "It is proper to avoid such people and not to speak about them in private or in public" (*Letter to the Smyrneans* 7:2).

96 An encouragement to follow Jesus's teaching in Mt 6:2-18.

97 Lit., "the time of your faith."

98 Greek had two words for "time": *chronos* was time in general; *kairos* meant "a moment in time." Both words are used in this verse. The "time [*chronos*] of your faith" means a time span. The "last moment in time [*kairos*]" means the exact moment of the *eschaton*. By growing in faith, the Christian grows in perfection, which is

will be increased and sheep will be turned into wolves and love will be turned into hate.[99] (4) As lawlessness grows, they will hate, persecute, and betray one another, and then the world deceiver will appear as a son of God and will perform signs and wonders, and the earth will be delivered into his hands, and he will do unlawful things that have never been done. (5) Then the creation of men will come to the burning of trial [judgment]. Many will be scandalized[100] and perish, but those who endure in their faith will be saved by him who became the curse.[101] (6) Then the signs of truth will appear. The first is a sign spreading out in heaven,[102] then a sign of the trumpet blast, and the third the resurrection of the dead. (7) But not for all, as it was said, "The Lord and all his holy ones will come with him." (8) Then the world will see the Lord coming on the clouds of heaven.

---

always the goal of the spiritual life.

99 Mt 24:12: "Because of the increase of lawlessness, the love of many will grow cold."

100 I.e., "will fall away," as Holmes translates it.

101 There is a wide range of translations and opinions about the meaning of the Didachist's words. I follow Rordorf and Holmes in identifying Christ as the accursed one who took the malediction (curse) for believers. This is in line with Paul's statement in Gal 3:13, "Christ redeemed us from the curse of the law by becoming a curse for us." In the early church, Christians were asked to curse Christ — something that lies behind 1 Cor 12:3: "Jesus is accursed." See also the advice given to Polycarp, "As the proconsul was insistent, he said, 'Swear and I will release you. Revile Christ!' But Polycarp said, 'I have served him eighty-six years, and he has done me no wrong. How can I blaspheme my King who saved me?'" *Martyrdom of Polycarp* 9:3.

102 The meaning of *semeion ekpetaseos* "a sign spreading out in heaven" is not clear. Rordorf sees this as evoking the cross, whose arms are open to embrace the world.

Bibliography

Bauer, Walter, William Arndt, and F. Wilbur Gingrich. *A Lexicon of the New Testament and Other Early Christian Literature*. Chicago: University of Chicago Press, 1952.

Beyschlag, Karlmann. *Clemens Romanus und der Frühkatholizismus. Untersuchungen zu I Clemens 1-7*. Tübingen: Mohr, 1966.

Breytenback, C., and L.L. Welborn, eds. *Encounters with Hellenism: Studies on the First Letter of Clement*. Arbeiten zur Geschichte des antiken Judentums und Urchristentums 53. Leiden / Boston: Brill, 2004.

Ehrman, Bart, ed. and trans. *The Apostolic Fathers*. Cambridge, MA: Harvard University Press, 2003.

Finn, Thomas M. "Review: A Church in Crisis: Ecclesiology and Paraenesis in Clement of Rome." *Catholic Biblical Quarterly* 53, no. 3 (Jul 1991): 490.

Grant, Robert. *The Apostolic Fathers: A New Translation and Commentary*. Vol. 2, *First and Second Clement*. New York: Thomas Nelson & Sons, 1965.

Hammond, C.E. *Antient Liturgies*. Reprint, Piscataway, NJ: Gorgias Press, 2004.

Hemmer, Hippolyte. *Clément de Rome: Épître aux Corinthiens et Homélie du IIe siècle*. Les Pères Apostoliques. Paris: Libraire Alphonse Picard et fils, 1909.

Holmes, Michael W., ed. and trans. *The Apostolic Fathers: Greek Texts and English Translations*. 3rd ed. 1992. Reprint, Grand Rapids: Baker Academic, 2007.

Howell, Kenneth J. *Ignatius of Antioch and Polycarp of Smyrna: A New Translation and Theological Commentary*. Zanesville, OH: CHResources, 2009.

Jaubert, Annie. *Clément de Rome: Épître aux Corinthiens.* Sources Chrétiennes 167. Paris: Éditions du Cerf, 1971.

Jurgens, W.A. *Faith of the Early Fathers.* Collegeville: Order of St. Benedict, Inc., 1970.

Kleist, James. *The Epistles of St. Clement of Rome and St. Ignatius of Antioch.* Ancient Christian Writers 1. Mahwah: Paulist Press, 1946.

Knopf, Rudolf. *Die Lehre der zwölf Apostel, Die zwei Clemensbriefe.* Tübingen: J.C.B. Mohr, 1920.

Lake, Krisopp. *The Apostolic Fathers.* Vol. 1, *Clement.* 1912. Reprint, London: William Heinemann, 1970.

Lampe, G.W.H., ed. *A Greek Patristic Lexicon.* Oxford: Oxford University Press, 1961.

Lightfoot, J.B. *The Apostolic Fathers: Clement, Ignatius, and Polycarp.* Vols. 1 and 2. 1887. Reprint, Peabody: Hendrickson Publishers, 1989.

Louth, Andrew, and Maxwell Staniforth. *Early Christian Writings: The Apostolic Fathers.* New York: Putnam Inc., 1968.

Meyendorff, John. *The Primacy of Peter: Essays in Ecclesiology and the Early Church.* Paris: St. Vladimir's Seminary Press, 1992.

Quacquarelli, Antonio. *I Padri Apostolici.* Rome: Citta Nuova Editrice, 1976.

Rordorf, Willy, and André Tulier. *La Doctrine des Douze Apôtres.* Sources Chrétiennes no. 248bis. Paris: Éditions du Cerf, 1978.

Sanders, Louis. *L'héllénisme de Saint Clément de Rome et le Paulinisme.* Studia Hellenistica. Lovanii: Bibliotheca Universitatis, 1943.

Unnik, W.C. Van. "Is 1 Clement 20 Purely Stoic?" *Vigiliae Christianae* 4, no. 3 (Jul 1950): 181-189.

Young, F.W. "The Relation of 1 Clement to the Epistle of James." *Journal of Biblical Literature* 67 (1948): 339-345.

Index of Principal Greek Terms

Explanation: The reader should keep in mind that the translations given below are only indicators of the general meaning. In some contexts, these words can be translated with different English words. Since Greek verbs can have many inflected forms, I have listed them below as they usually appear in dictionaries (lexicons) of ancient Greek.

abanausos (beyond-perfunctory service) 117n204
agape (love) 29, 47, 72n5
aischrologos (shameful, foul language) 140n26
akontes (unwillingly) 81n10
alazoneia (bragging, arrogance) 143n47
aletheia (truth) 51
amnesikakos (forgiving) 81n13
amomos (blameless, without stain) 138n14
aphiemi (forgive) 146n61
archiereus (high priest) 40n4
asthenes (weak, feeble) 85n32
atenizo (stare, gaze, fix one's eyes) 43, 86n36, 97n93
athoos (blameless or innocent) 138n14
athumia (discouragement, despair) 119n218

banausos (mechanical, a matter of duty) 117n204

charis (grace) 138n7
charisma (gift) 138n13
charizomai (give graciously) 74
cheirotoneo (elect, appoint) 151n93
chrestotes (goodness, kindness) 87n44
christemporos (using Christ for personal gain) 150n86
Christos (Christ) 150n86
chronos (time, duration of time) 151n98

demiourgos (Creator) 38
despotes (Master) 37
diadechomai (succeed to e.g. an office) 117n203
didache (teaching, instruction) 137–152 inter alia
didomi (give) 74
dikaioo (justify) 105n140
dikaiosune (justice, righteousness) 51
dipsuchos (double-minded) 89n55

eis (into, unto, with a view to, on behalf of, for) 69, 70, 134n292
ekklesia (church) 67, 69–71, 143n40
emporos (salesman) 150n86
epanapauo (to rest on, to rely on) 141n31
epi (above, on, over) 145n59
epieikeia (forbearance, pliability) 134n289
epimone (provision?) 117n202
epiousios (daily, supersubstantial) 145n59
episkope (position of overseer, bishop's office) 26n4, 28
episkopos (bishop) 27–28, 130n271
eris (strife) 18
eschatos (last) 61, 139n15, 151n98
ethnos (nation, Gentile, pagan) 138n8
eucharisteo (give thanks, hold Eucharist) 72, 146n63, 147n69, 148n77, 150n89
eucharistia (thanksgiving, Eucharist) 68, 72, 146n63
euergesia (kindness, benefit) 112n179
exairetos (precious, chosen) 145n59

hamartia (sin) 132n282
hegemonikos (guiding, leading) 96n91
hemera (day) 64
hesuchia (quiet, silence) 91n63
homonoia (harmony, united mind) 19n5, 88n49
hosanna (hosanna, save now) 148, 148n75
huperidete (despise) 151n94

hupselophthalmos (lit. high eye, wandering eyes) 140n26
hydor (water) 144n54

kairos (time, moment, opportunity) 101n119, 151n98
kakia (evil, malice) 143n44
kakologeo (use abusive language) 140n23
kallistos (beautiful, illustrious) 84n30
katoikeo (reside in a country i.e. as a citizen) 79n1. *See paroikeo.*
klasma (broken bread) 68
kleos (renown) 49
kosmos (cosmos, world) 96n93
kuophoreo (give birth) 97n98
kurios (Lord) 37n1
kuriotes (lordship) 141n29

laos periousios (special people) 134n292
leitourgia (liturgy, public service) 113n187

metanoia (conversion, repentance, change of mind or heart) 48, 86n39, 133n287
musterion (mystery) 69–71
musterion kosmikon (mystery in the world) 69, 71

opheile (debt) 146n60
opheilema (debt) 146n60
ousios (substantial, of an essence) 145n59

paideia (correction, instruction) 109n159
paideuo (teach, instruct, train) 130n272
pais (child, servant, beloved servant) 73, 129n265, 146n65
paliggenesia (restoration, rebirth) 88n48
paradosis (tradition, passing on of an office) 28, 85n35
paraggelia (command, precept) 115n194
paratheke (deposit) 28
paroikeo (sojourn, live as a resident alien) 79n1
parousia (presence, coming, arrival) 61, 147n74

pepoithesis (confidence, trust) 47

periousios (special, peculiar) 134n292, 145n59

pharmakeuo (give drugs, engage in sorcery) 139n20

pharmakia (administration of drugs, sorcery) 143n43

phaulos (simple, slight, insignificant; bad, evil, base) 103n132

philoxenia (hospitality) 19n6

phthonos (envy) 24n1

pisteuo (believe, trust) 46, 46n3

pistis (faith) 46, 51

pistos (faithful) 132n281

pistoo (entrust with) 115n195

platusmos (expansion, scope, growth) 82n16

plemmeleia (fault, sin) 132n282

pneumatikos (spiritual, of the Spirit) 120n220

poieo (do, make, practice) 105n144

poimaino (rule, shepherd) 124n245

poimen (shepherd) 19

politeia (citizenship) 81n15

politeuomai (live or behave as a free citizen) 84n29

praxis (lifestyle, deed, practice) 105n143

presbuteros (presbyter, elder) 120n223

propempo (send ahead, help on the way) 51n5

prosklisis (proclivities, inclination, partiality) 120n221,
    122n235

schisma (division) 15–16

semeion (sign) 89n56, 152n102

semeiosis (signifying) 89n56

semeron (today) 64

sophia (wisdom, understanding) 107n150

sophrosune (discretion, thinking soberly) 133n288

sozo (save, preserve) 111n174

splagchnon (lit. bowels, metaphorically = inner heart,) 80n6

stasiazo (foment rebellion or sedition) 17n2

stasis (rebellion, sedition) 17–18

sugkatabasis (condescension, the act of coming down) 39

sunesis (understanding, wisdom) 107n150
sunoche (prison) 139n16

tagma (order, proper place) 114n191
telos (purpose, goal, end) 49
temeleo (care for, look after) 111n176
theos (God) 37
thrasos (audacity, arrogance) 141n27
threskeia (religion, worship) 133n286
tupos (type, stamp) 142n38

zelos (jealousy) 24n1
zelotupia (jealousy, rivalry, envy) 143n46

General Index

Note: Where the index points to a simple page number, the content may be found one or more times, anywhere in the body of the page and/or in multiple footnotes. A page number that is followed by an "n" and a second number (as in 118n211) is a special case that refers to a single specified note (#211) on the designated page (118).

A

Aaron
    and Miriam 83
    rod budded 116

Abbreviations vii–viii

Abednego 118n211

Abel 50, 82–83

Abiram, consequences of jealousy 83

Abraham 88, 105
    faith of 49–52, 54, 87n47, 88
    father 39n3, 49, 51, 105
    friend of God 94
    hospitality commended 19, 50, 89

Abuse
    abusive language 140
    liturgical abuse 15–16

Achaia, setting of Corinth 2

Acts of the Apostles
    appointment of ordained pastors 26, 114n191, 151n93
    Clement quote re David after God's heart 95n89
    giving rather than receiving 80n5
    history 1, 13–14
    outreach to Gentiles 27
    prayer at fixed hours 146n62

Adam 39n3, 85, 104, 122

Alexandria 129n267
    Apollos of 8, 15, 17, 120
    Clement of 9, 11, 59, 66
    Origen of 122n233

Anacletus preceded Clement as bishop of Rome 6

Ananias *See* Shadrach

Angels 41, 104, 108, 110, 113, 129n267, 141n30

Antioch
    Ignatius of i, vii, 13, 29, 31–32, 68, 84n27, 117n206,
        146n66, 151n95, 153
    Theophilus of 58

Apostolic succession 3, 21, 23, 25–26, 28, 30–31, 35, 117n203

Apollinaris of Laodicea 122n233

Apollos, *See* Apollos of Alexandria

Aquila, native of Pontus, resident in Corinth 14

Arabia 101–102

Areopagus, site of sermon by apostle Paul in Athens 14

Arrogance
    avoid 4n7, 20, 99, 104, 109, 127
    contrast to humility of Christ 19, 53, 93
    contrast to love 121
    Lord humbles the arrogant 129

Asia Minor, 9, 11, 30–31

Athanasius, author of Festal Letter 59

Athens, *See* Areopagus

Atlantic Ocean and Atlantis 98n103

Attitudes
    base 103, 121
    bragging 143n47
    insufficient to justify 47
    servant attitude 4
    toward ordained leaders 49

Augustine 139n17

Aurelius, Marcus, author of *Meditations* 103n134

Author, Clement as author of letter 4–7

Authority
    Paul's letters 17, 111n173, 115n193
    primacy of Rome 10, 23–35
    See also structure

Autolycus 58n3

Azariah *See* Meschach

B

Barnabas, Epistle of 59, 62

Bathsheba 95n88, 96n92

Belief 46, 50, 52, 77

Beyond–perfunctory service 21, 117

Bishop
    appointment of 24, 61, 115, 151n93
    holy behavior of 25, 28, 117
    of Rome 2, 5–7, 9–11, 30–32
    office of 24–25, 26n4, 27–30, 79n3, 117
    overseer 26n4, 130

Biton, Valerius 135

Blameless behavior
    exhortation 9, 80–81, 138
    unity, not division 122

Blessing of God 47, 51, 63, 88, 105, 107–108, 123

Blood of Christ 42–43, 74, 85, 86n36, 99, 122

Body
    mystical body (the church) 111
    of Christ 3, 23, 43, 74, 111n175, 122n232
    of presbyters 28
    unity of the one body 68, 111, 119, 138n13

Bread
    broken bread 67–68, 71, 74, 146
    Christ's presence in 16, 145n59

daily bread 64, 107, 145
Eucharist 71, 74, 76, 132n283, 150

Bryennios, Philotheos, in 1873 rediscovered the *Didache* 57

C

Cain, 50, 82–83

Call
abandoning God's call 89n55
to faith and holiness 3, 5, 19, 46, 99, 106
to manifest love of God 23
to ordained ministry 54, 93n74
to serve as soldiers 110n169
to unity, submission to rightful authority 16, 116n201

Catholic perspective ii–iii, 29, 105n140, 132n283

Cephas 8, 15, 17, 120
See also Peter

Chosen by God 19n4, 104n135, 116, 123, 134n292

Christ
and his flock 4, 19–25, 53, 93, 117, 125, 127
and humility 4, 19–21, 53–54, 93
blood of 42–43, 74, 85, 86n36, 99, 122
Clement's view of 37–44
high priest 40–43, 76, 109, 133
manifests divine love 3, 23, 35, 37, 40–44, 122
See also God, Jesus

Chrysostom, John 129n267

Church
and the *Didache* 58–59, 67–71
apostolic 3, 10, 16, 23, 33
history 1, 5–6
in Rome 1–2, 5–6, 10–11, 23, 26, 30–35, 51, 79, 84
See unity, harmony

Cicero 97n95

Citizen 79n1, 81n15, 84n29

Claudius
>   Emperor of Rome 14
>   Claudius Ephebus 135

Clement of Alexandria, author of *Stromata* 9, 11

Clement of Rome
>   dependence on Letter to the Hebrews 24, 40–42, 50,
>   109n163, 110n165
>   mentioned by apostle Paul 6
>   view of the church 23–35
>   view of God and Christ 37–44
>   *See Letter of Clement to the Corinthians*

Conduct 9, 21, 80–81, 120, 123, 125, 141

Confidence 81, 102, 115
>   from God's goodness 47, 81, 102, 107–108, 115
>   from the blood of the cross 42
>   from the resurrection 24
>   Isaac and 105–106
>   *See also* hope

Constantinople 57, 122n233, 129n267

Conversion, change of heart and mind 48, 86n39, 133

Corinth
>   sedition and schism in church at 13–22
>   city of 1–2, 5–7, 81n8
>   letter of Clement to 10

Correcting one another 69, 109, 126

Covenant
>   continuity between old and new 37, 41
>   failure to maintain 92, 109
>   God to be worshiped by all nations 131n277
>   *See also* new covenant

Creator
>   adoration of 96, 107–108, 112, 134
>   order, unity 48, 98
>   power, transcendence 37–39, 102, 129–130
>   the only God 10

Crete, island of 27

D

Daily bread 64, 145

Danaids 49, 84–85

Daniel, persecution of righteous man 118

Dates (years a.d.)
    50 Paul's arrival in Corinth 14
    50–150 writing of the *Didache* 65–66
    64 great fire of Rome under Nero 84n31
    70 destruction of temple in Jerusalem 114n192
    81 to 96 Domitian was Emperor of Rome 80
    90–100 Clement's *Letter to the Corinthians* 2
    93 Clement became bishop of Rome 6
    107–108 letters of Ignatius of Antioch 13, 146n66
    108 martyrdom of Ignatius of Antioch 29
    135 Polycarp's *Letter to the Philippians* 8n14
    180 writings of Irenaeus of Lyons 33
    325 Nicene formulation of Trinity 128n264
    1873 rediscovery of the *Didache* 57

Dathan, consequences of jealousy 83

David, King 72–73, 83, 95, 124, 146, 148

Death, way of, section of *Didache* 60, 137, 143–144

Deeds
    base, lawless 93, 103
    good, glorious 96, 105n143, 112, 121, 140, 151

Deposit of faith 28

Didache
    and ancient church 58–59
    and contemporary church 67–71
    and Gospel of Matthew 60–66
    and Syria 58
    church order section 148–151
    date written 65–66
    Didachist 57–77, 137n2, 144–147, 150n92

English translation 137–152
Eucharist 72–74
Eucharist as sacrifice 74–77
final things section 151–152
four sections 60
history and literature 57–66
liturgical section 144–148
rediscovery of 57
theology of 67–77
unity, one writer or many 59–62
ways of life and death section 137–144

Dionysius, bishop, writer of letters to Soter, 6–7, 11, 32, 34–35

Dircae 49, 84–85

Division *See* sedition and schism

Domitian, Emperor of Rome 6, 79n3

Discretion, virtue of 42, 48–49, 133, 135

Double-minded 39–40, 89, 100, 141

Drugs, harmful 139–140, 143n43

E

Easter festal letters 34

Egypt 83, 95, 102, 124

Ehrman, Bart vi–vii, 30–31, 70, 81n12, 87n44, 93n77, 101n119, 115n195, 142–143, 148–149, 151

Elders 3, 17, 82, 120n223, 126

Eleutherius, bishop of Rome 33

Elect
    chosen of God 4n8, 17, 40, 47–48, 80–81, 84, 104, 119, 121–122, 128–129, 151
    Matthias elected to replace Judas 26

Elijah and Elisha 94

Enoch 87

Envy and jealousy
    and anger 134
    history of 82–85, 116, 118
    lead to death 3–4, 63, 82, 87, 113, 143
    lead to strife 15, 17–18, 24, 50, 82, 91, 140
Ephebus, Claudius 135
Ephesians
    and Paul 27, 80n4
    Letter to, from Ignatius of Antioch 68, 146n66
Ephesus 27, 30
Epictetus, Stoic philosopher 103n132
Esau 83
Esther, "perfect in faith" 48, 126
Eucharist
    and the *Didache* 60, 72–74
    liturgy in the church 16, 29, 43, 67–68, 122n232
    sacrifice and the *Didache* 71–77, 117n206, 144–147
Eusebius, bishop of Caesarea 5–7, 9, 28, 34–35, 59

F

Faith
    and repentance 48–49
    and virtue 19n6, 52–55
    and works 46, 49–52
    Christian ii–iii, 1
    Clement's view 45–55
    purpose and practice 9–10, 22, 32, 49
    See also faithful
Faithful
    faithfulness to earlier tradition 27–28, 33
    God faithful to his promises 102, 131–132
    God's people 5, 10, 24, 59, 85, 127
    Jesus, high priest 40
    obedience 50, 88, 95, 116, 121
Family relations 9, 53, 88, 130n273

Fasting 60, 63, 124, 126, 138, 145

Flock 4, 19–25, 53–54, 93, 117, 125, 127

Forgiveness
> God grants 39, 123, 125, 132, 148
> we petition 64, 125, 146
> relating to one another 81, 91

Fortunatus 135

France *See* Irenaeus

G

Gaul *See* Irenaeus

Gallio, Roman proconsul 14

Gaze, fix eyes on things of God 41, 43, 86n36, 87, 94, 96, 110

Gift
> through sacraments 28, 117
> differing gifts 111
> what God gives 16, 35, 40, 45, 47, 97, 100, 106, 108, 112n180, 123n244, 138–139
> what we offer 25, 43, 74–75

God
> almighty Father 37–40
> Clement's view of 37–44
> compassionate 37, 39, 95
> eternal 126, 135, 139
> holiness of 39, 107, 128 *See also* Holy Spirit
> incomprehensible 107
> just 86n37, 96
> knowable 35, 124, 131
> knowledge of 73
> merciful 40, 51, 87n45, 95, 122, 130n274, 131, 133
> order 37, 46
> provident/ providence 38, 39, 47, 97n25, 101, 107n151, 130n274
> truth 95, 132
> wisdom of 89, 96, 107n150, 131
> *See also* Jesus, Christ, Holy Spirit

Grace
    completely free gift 47, 73–74, 138
    of God 4, 19, 37, 39, 52, 100, 105, 111n173, 122, 130n273,
        147
    of repentance 43, 86
    salutation or farewell 79, 135
    to the humble 130n268
    unity and 119
    women, empowered 125
    yoke of Christ 20, 53–54, 94
Grant, Robert vi–vii, 82n16, 85n32, 97n96, 111n174,
        117n204, 120n221, 122n235, 130n272
Greco–Roman culture 111n171
Guidance
    by God 23, 38, 96–97
    through faith and prayer 26, 50, 137n2
    through church structure 35, 53, 113n186, 132–134

H

Hades 83, 124
Harmony *See* unity
Heart
    change of heart and mind 48, 81, 86–87, 96, 110, 127–
        129, 133n287, 147
    God searches the 98–99, 132
    right disposition of ii, 8, 41, 46–47, 54, 71, 73, 77, 80, 95,
        106, 144
    wrong disposition of 48, 82, 92, 123–124
Hebrew
    and Greek expressions 134n292, 145n59, 148n75
    language and Greek Septuagint 75, 82n20, 86n39, 91n63,
        94n78, 96
    tradition 60, 104
    universality inherited by church 131n277
Hegesippus, author of lost 2nd century history 6, 11, 28, 35

Heliopolis, city in Egypt 102

Hemmer, Hippolyte vii, 96n91, 117n204, 120n221

Hermes, Shepherd of, spurious writing 59

High priest
  Jesus 40–43, 76, 109, 133, 135
  Levitical 114, 150

History
  Didache 57–66
  early church i–iii, 1, 13–14, 5–11, 35
  Eusebius 5–7, 9, 28, 34–35, 59
  guided by God 38, 42

Hittite, *See* Uriah the Hittite

Holiness
  call to 3–5, 19, 40, 46–47, 72, 86, 92, 99, 102, 104, 106,
    108, 119, 121, 132–133

Holmes, Michael vi–vii, 70, 82n16, 87n44, 101n119, 104–107,
    109n157, 111, 114n190, 117–118, 120n221, 122n235,
    132–133, 139–143, 149–152

Holofernes, killed heroically by Judith 126

Holy people 73, 86, 86n40

Holy Spirit 24, 28, 53, 81, 86, 90, 93, 96, 99, 115, 118, 128,
    134, 144

  See also God

Hope
  confidence 24, 42, 47, 81, 102, 105–108, 115, 128
  God is our hope 29, 47–48, 90, 94, 129, 142
  perfected through love and worship 22, 29, 100, 115
  perseverance in 21, 118, 127

Hosanna *See* Greek index

Hospitality
  Abraham 50, 88–89
  essential practice 3, 19, 23, 80
  Rahab 50, 89n53

Humility
    Clement exhorts to 4, 19–21, 80, 90–91, 93–96, 99, 105,
        112, 121, 141
    God raises the humble 129–130
    Judith 126
    leaders in the church 21, 25, 117
    Moses 124
    of forefathers 48, 134
    virtue of 52–55, 128, 144n49

I

Ignatius of Antioch 84n27, 153
    Eucharist 72, 117n206, 146n66
    letters of i, vii–viii, 13, 29, 151n95
    offices of bishop and presbyter 27
    primacy of Rome 31–32
    structure of church 30
    unity of church 68, 146n66

Innocence 92, 119, 129, 138n14

Instruction
    of the young 9, 99
    received 10
    re procedure 61
    re worship, godliness 16, 59, 65, 133–134, 143
    submit to 8, 53, 109, 127

Irenaeus
    and Clement's Letter 9–10
    apostolic succession 28, 117n203
    bishop of Lyons in Gaul (France) 11, 33–34
    primacy of Rome 30, 33–34, 84

Isaac, sacrifice of 50, 89n54, 105–106

Isaiah
    humility of Christ 4, 20, 53, 54
    vine imagery 72–73

Israel
    allotment of God's inheritance 104, 134n292

and repentance 86
continuity and the church 37, 41, 72
leaders to be honored 116, 126
patriarchs of 106
psalms and praise 60
unity the intention of God 92n66

J

Jacob
and Esau 83
humility 106
Jeshurun forsook God 82n17
the Lord's portion 104

James the apostle, and justification 45–46, 49–52, 89

Jaubert, Annie vi–vii, 8n14, 45n1, 87n44, 90n60, 98n103,
101n119, 105–106, 109n157, 111, 114, 115n195,
117–118, 120–123, 125n252

Jealousy
See envy

Jericho 53, 89–90

Jerome, *Commentary on Matthew* 145n59

Jerusalem
Codex Hierosolymitanus 57
Jesus's entry into 148n75
temple sacrifice 76, 114

Jeshurun *See* Jacob

Jesse, father of King David 95

Jesus (found on 56 pages)
"your child Jesus" 73–74, 129–131, 146–147
See also God, Christ

Jew
Aquila 14
Dialogue with Trypho the Jew 76

Jewish
affinity to "Two Ways" 62

law and regulations 14, 46

milieu and culture 76, 111n171, 137n2, 145n56, 147n68, 148n75

tradition 45n1, 50, 65, 104n136, 141n32

vices to be avoided 139n18

Job 95, 102

Jonah and the Ninevites 86

Joseph and jealousy of his brothers 83

Joshua *See* Rahab

Judaism 51, 60, 137n2
See also Jewish

Judaizers 51–52

Judas, replacement as disciple by Matthias 26

Judith 126

Justification
doctrine of 45–52, 94, 105–106
God is justified in his pronouncements 95
old covenant basis for the new 41

Justin Martyr 58, 66, 72, 76, 90

K

Kindness
kindness of God 38–40, 87n44, 94n81, 98, 100, 112, 132
let us be kind 91

Kleist, James vi–vii, 81n11m, 82n16, 87n44, 104n138, 105n140, 111n174, 117n204, 118n209, 120n221, 121n224, 123n243

Knopf, Rudolf 45n1

L

Laban and humility of Jacob 106

Lake, Kirsopp 70

Laodicea 82n18, 122n233

Leaders

line of Judah 106
presbyters, bishops 27, 30, 49, 80, 99
schism and sedition against 15, 18, 123–124
respecting 55, 80, 99n109, 110–111, 114n191, 116, 133

Lebanon, cedars of 91

Letter of Clement to the Corinthians
English translation 79–135
in history of early church 5–11
parallels to Polycarp's *Letter to the Philippians* 8–9
what letter is about i, 2–5, 17, 19, 45

Levitical order 41, 106, 114n188, 116n201

Life, way of, section of *Didache* 60, 137–144

Lightfoot, J.B., Anglican bishop of Durham vi, viii, 8, 84n31,
104n136, 111n176, 118n209, 125n252, 127n262,
129n266

Liturgy
abuses against 15
established, orderly 16, 98, 108n155, 113–114
eucharistic 43, 73
liturgical language 5, 38, 41, 65–66, 97n96, 129–132,
150n90
section of *Didache* 60–61, 67–68, 72, 143–148

Logos, eternal 122n233

Lord's Prayer 61, 63–65, 145n58

Lot 19n6, 87n47, 88–89

Love
foundation for unity 11, 16, 19–23, 120–123
God's 39–40, 68–69, 81n9, 91n63
Jesus the manifestation of divine love 28, 32, 40–44, 130,
144n49
nature of the church iii, 2–3, 5, 11, 35, 37, 98n104
works of love 9, 47–48, 52, 62, 69, 95, 99, 106, 125, 126,
133, 137–141

Luke 14, 64–65

LXX *See* Septuagint

Lyons *See* Irenaeus

M

Magnificat of Mary 130n268

Malachi
    quoted by Didachist 74–77
    quoted by Justin 76

Maranatha 148

Marcus *See* Aurelius

Mark 54, 129n267

Martyr *See* Justin, *also* martyrdom

Martyrdom
    of Clement of Rome 9
    of Danaids and Dircae 84n31
    of Ignatius of Antioch 29
    of Peter and Paul 2, 4, 49, 84n27
    of Polycarp 8, 68, 152n101
    of Pothinus (predecessor of Eusebius) 34

Massoretic Text (MT) viii, 75, 82n20, 83n21, 127n260

Matthew
    Clement and 54
    Didache and 60–66, 74–75
    Jerome's *Commentary on Matthew* 145n59
    Justin and 58n5

Matthias and apostolic succession 26

Meshach 118n211

Messiah 104n137

Milavec, Aaron vi, 61, 62n9, 67n1, 70, 137n1, 139n17,
    149n80, 151n93

Miriam, sister of Moses 83

Mishael *See* Abednego

Moses 83, 95, 116, 123–125

Mount *See* Sermon on the Mount

Mystery of the church, "performing" the 69–72, 149

N

Nathan, prophet to David 95n88

Nicene Creed 128n264

Nero, Emperor of Rome 84n31

New covenant
    church as God's inheritance 104n138, 135
    Jesus high priest of new 40–42, 51, 114n188
    See also covenant

Ninevites and Jonah 86

Noah 86–87

O

Obedience
    examples 50, 88–89, 96, 106n146, 109n157
    to God 87–88, 91, 128, 134
    to presbyters 5, 8, 18, 110–111, 121n229
    structure and authority 22, 48

Office *See* bishop

Order
    in the church 3–5, 23–24, 48–49, 54, 113–115, 118n208
    levitical 41
    nature of God and his creation 37, 40, 46, 107, 129n266
    section of the *Didache* 60–61, 148–151

Origen of Alexandria 122n233

P

Pagan
    civil system 14, 84–85
    religion 2, 4n6, 16, 76, 102n121, 144n50
    society 2, 21, 68, 138, 139n19

Paul the apostle
    and Clement 6, 21, 25, 46–47, 80n4, 91n61, 99, 108n156,
        109n162, 111–112, 114, 119n215
    as authority 8
    faith and works 45, 49–52, 89n54, 105n140
    history 1–2, 4, 13–19, 27–28, 84, 85n35
    letters of 7, 27, 68, 72n6, 74, 81, 82n19, 110n164, 115n193
    primacy of Rome 10, 26, 33

Peace
    and justice 17, 48, 82
    and harmony 10, 19, 23–24, 34, 38, 48, 88n49, 131n279,
        134–135
    and love 3, 98, 100, 151
    and rule by presbyters 20, 92, 125, 141
    gift of God 42, 79, 81, 93, 96–97, 127, 132–133

Peter
    apostolic succession 5, 25–26, 31, 33
    endurance of 84
    epistles of 19n4, 47, 79, 135, 141n29
    history 2, 4, 15, 49
    primacy of Rome 10, 33
    spurious *Apocalypse of Peter* 59
    the See of iii
    See also martyrdom of Peter and Paul

Pharaoh 124

Philadelphia in Asia Minor, Ignatius's letter to 30

Philippians *See* Polycarp

Phoenix, legend of 4n6, 101, 102

Pilgrim people 5, 19, 79, 119, 147n74

Pius XII, *Mystici Corporis Christi* 111n175

Polycarp
    Eusebius and 33, 84n27
    Letter to the Philippians vii, 7–9, 99n107, 138n9, 141n32
    martyrdom 68, 152n101
    parallels to Clement's letter 8–9, 99n107

Pope 30, 132n283

Pothinus *See* martyrdom

Preface i–iii

Presbyters
    blessed 117
    disobedience to 53, 87n46, 120
    extension of levitical order 41
    obedience and honor to 8, 49, 80, 99, 127
    properly appointed 20, 24–25, 27–29, 125

Protestant ii, 11, 105n140, 120n223

Public reading of letters 6–7, 9, 35

Q

Quacquarelli, Antonio vi, viii, 70, 84n31, 116n200, 118n209,
    120n221, 151n93

Quiet, silence 21, 25, 91, 92, 93, 99, 109, 117, 128, 141

Qumran 143n40

R

Rahab 19n6, 42, 50, 53–54, 87n47, 89–90

Rebellion *See* sedition and schism

Repentance
    broken and contrite spirit 86n37, 96, 124
    call to 3, 8, 86–87, 127, 148, 151
    change of mind and heart 48, 133n287
    gift from God 43–44

Resurrection
    confidence through the 24, 115
    future 101–102, 152
    pagans and idea of 4n6

Restoration of peace, unity ii, 5, 20, 48, 88, 120, 127

Righteousness
    accounted righteous 50, 87–88, 94

call to 48, 60, 83–84, 91–92, 100, 105, 107, 113, 118, 121,
    126, 133, 137n2, 143, 148
gift of God 47, 106, 131
Rome (Roman)
    authorities in the empire 4, 14
    bishops 5–7, 9–11, 30–32
    city of 1–2
    Coliseum 85n34
    church and apostles 17, 26n3, 26, 50, 51, 84
    holy citizens 84n29
    liturgy 41, 43, 97n96
    primacy and succession 9–10, 23–35
Rordorf, Willy vi, viii, 58n2, 59n6, 61, 66, 70, 72, 139n17,
    140n26, 142n29, 143, 145n57, 146n63, 149n80,
    151n93, 152n101

S

Sabaoth, Lord of 108

Sacrifice and the Eucharist 44, 71, 74–77, 117n206, 150

Salvation 24, 37, 40, 43, 45–55

Saul, King of Israel 83

Schism *See* sedition and schism

Second coming or return of Christ 61, 88, 147n74

Sedition and schism
    division in the church 2, 7, 15–16, 18, 22, 82n18, 119–122
    in Israel 83, 116, 123
    love is the opposite 22
    sedition in the church at Corinth 3–4, 6, 13–22
    schism and rebellion 5, 17–18, 48, 52–53, 80, 87n46,
        92n66, 115n193

Septuagint (abbreviation LXX) viii, 75, 82, 83n21, 86n39,
    90n57, 91n63, 94–96, 100, 104n136, 113n182,
    115n197, 119n213, 121n228, 124n245, 127n260,
    145n59

Sermon on the Mount 60, 62–63, 69

Servant
    attitude 4, 86n38, 142
    Jesus as servant 73, 93n75, 129n265
    people 15, 72–73, 83, 112, 116, 123–125, 132, 146

Shadrach 118n211

Shepherd of Hermes, spurious writing 59

Silence *See* quiet

Sin
    Christ the remedy 4, 40, 87, 93–94
    confession, repentance of 60, 71, 74, 86, 95–96, 114, 123,
        127, 132, 143, 150n90
    deadly 82n19, 83, 109, 112n178, 148
    inadvertent 81n10
    love covers 120, 121, 141
    of disunity 8, 123n242
    rejection of those in authority 25, 117, 125
    welcome to sinners 3

Smyrna, city in Asia Minor 30, 33–34
    See also Polycarp

Sodom and Lot 89

Sojourn *See* pilgrim people

Sola fide 45n1

Sorceries *See* drugs, harmful

Soter, letter from Dionysius 6–7, 34

Spain and the apostle Paul 1, 51

Stoic philosophy 97n95, 103

Strife *See* sedition and schism, *see also* envy

Stromata See Clement of Alexandria

Structure of the church 2–3, 5, 20–35, 37, 92n67

Substantial, supersubstantial 145n59

Syria 58

T

Teach the young 9, 80, 100, 142

Thanks, thanksgiving 68, 72–73, 111–112, 114n190, 146–148, 150n89

Theophilus of Antioch 58

Timothy and a body of presbyters 28

Titus and church structure 27–28

Tradition
    apostolic 10, 33, 58
    Catholic, Orthodox, Protestant ii
    Jewish 45n1, 50, 60, 106n145
    liturgical 16, 72
    oral 25, 66
    something passed down 7, 27–28, 62, 65, 85, 90n58, 99n109, 128n264

Trallians, Letter to the 29

Trinity, three Persons 47, 96n90, 128n264, 144n53, 147n70

Trypho, *Dialogue with Trypho the Jew* 76, 90n58

U

Unity
    and repentance 48–49
    desire for ii
    harmony of the church iii, 5, 11, 15, 16, 19–20, 22–24, 34–35, 38, 68–69, 71, 80n4, 88, 91n64, 92n66, 97–98, 100n113, 105, 108, 111n173, 119n215, 121, 122n236, 123, 131n279, 132, 134–135, 140n24, 146n66, 147n74
    of a document 59
    of God 18

Uriah the Hittite, husband of Bathsheba 96n92

V

Valerius *See* Biton

Virtue
    endurance 21, 47, 84, 102, 108, 118, 135

faith gives birth to virtues 47, 49, 52–55, 80
hospitality 3, 19, 23, 80, 89
piety 46–47, 92n67, 106
priesthood as means to virtue 42
See also humility

W

Water, running or living 144–145

Weakness 40–41, 49, 85, 93, 95, 109, 111, 131, 144n50

Wisdom
  asking God for 89n55
  God's 38, 95–96, 107, 127–128, 131–132
  Jewish wisdom tradition 45n1
  necessity of 3, 113, 128
  not source of justification 46–47, 90, 106
  of apostle Paul 8
  shown by good deeds 80, 112, 121, 134

Women 9
  empowered by God 125–126
  honored 9, 49, 80, 84–85, 90, 125
  See also Danaids, Dircae, Judith

Worship 16, 30, 39, 41, 60, 68–76, 95, 114–115, 118, 131n277,
    133n286

Y

Youth 3, 4n7, 9, 17, 80, 82, 84n31, 99, 104, 134, 139, 142

Z

Zahn, Theodor vi

About The Author

Kenneth J. Howell is Resident Theologian and Director of Pastoral Care of the Coming Home Network International. He is the author of seven books and has published dozens of articles in scholarly and popular journals. He taught for thirty years in seminaries and universities, most recently at the University of Illinois, Urbana-Champaign, and was simultaneously Director and Senior Fellow of the *St. John Institute of Catholic Thought* in Champaign. He has been a visiting professor at several universities, including Indiana University and the University of Sacramento. He has also lectured at the Universities of Notre Dame, Saint Thomas, and Iowa State University on the history of science and religion. His current research concentrates on the church fathers.

Acknowledgements

In a work of this kind, an author accumulates numerous debts of learning and friendship. Among the latter, I find myself highly appreciative of my colleagues and reviewers who have worked with me in the production of this book. Preeminently, Mary Clare Piecynski managed and edited the manuscript from its inception to its final form. Marie Jutras and Jeanette Flood, who offered expert editorial advice, gave of their time in a true spirit of service. Jim Anderson checked the translation carefully. Jennifer Bitler designed the internal layout and cover. Douglas Lowry prepared the indexes. Finally, Marcus Grodi has been a quiet but ever-faithful support for this project because of his belief that knowledge of the church fathers would enhance spiritual journeys of Christians in faith.